UNLOCK
THE
EINSTEIN
INSIDE

When a task is given in school, why does one student take thirty minutes to complete it and another only eight minutes?

In this book you'll come to understand the answer: students approach the task with varying learning tools. These tools are called cognitive skills, and these skills determine the quality, speed, and ease with which individuals learn and perform.

There can be factors other than weak cognitive skills, but recent studies by the National Institute of Health, the US Department of Education, and others indicate that the source of over 80% of learning problems is indeed weak cognitive skills.

I've written this book both to help you understand cognitive skills and to extend encouragement. Cognitive skills can be strengthened and improved, thereby reducing or eliminating learning and reading problems.

Eliminating learning problems is not just wishful thinking. In fact, our experience with over 15,000 students since 1995 demonstrates an average improvement of more than 3.6 years in learning skills and 4.6 years in reading skills—all in under 6 months (see Appendix C for 2005 results).

There is hope for any parent whose child struggles in school. The frustrations of falling behind in reading, math, and other areas of learning can come to an end with the appropriate cognitive skills training.

Your child can succeed in school and start a journey of learning that will result in a college education and a successful career. Believe it or not, there is a little "Einstein" locked up in every child, but to release it, you have to take the first step by having your child's cognitive skills assessed. The essential and critical next step is to strengthen the weak cognitive skills.

Thank you for your interest in this important subject and thank you for taking an interest in your child's education. Turn the page and take a look at how you can help your child become a better reader and a more successful student. Help your child gain the skills and tools necessary to become smarter...forever.

Dr. Ken Gibson

UNLOCK THE EINSTEIN INSIDE:

Applying New Brain Science
To Wake Up The Smart In Your Child

DR. KEN GIBSON

Unlock The Einstein Inside:
Applying New Brain Science To Wake Up The Smart In Your Child

Published By LearningRx™
5085 List Drive, Suite 200
Colorado Springs, Colorado 80919

Editorial services provided by Bruce Nygren, Melissa Tenpas, Larry McKnight,
and Bob Busha.

Publisher's Cataloging-in-Publication
(Provided by Quality Books, Inc.)

    Gibson, Ken, 1944-
      Unlock the Einstein inside : applying new brain
    science to wake up the smart in your child / Ken Gibson. -- 1st
    ed.
      p. cm.
      Includes bibliographical references.
      LCCN 2006927358
      ISBN-13: 978-1-4243-0480-6
      ISBN-10: 1-4243-0480-6

      1. Thought and thinking--Study and teaching.
    2. Cognitive learning. 3. Cognition in children.
    I. Title.

    LB1590.3.G54 2006   370.15'2
                    QBI06-600199

Library of Congress Control Number: 2006927358

Printed in the United States of America
2006—First Edition

10 9 8 7 6 5 4 3 2 1

This book is dedicated to the over fifteen thousand students
and parents who participated in our clinical trials, which focused on
developing solutions to learning and reading problems.
And, to the over eight hundred doctors, psychologists, educators—
and their staff members—who have contributed and worked with me
in testing and refining our cognitive training programs.

CONTENTS

1 : HOPE FOR EVERY CHILD

"I never teach my pupils; I only attempt to provide the conditions in which they can learn." — A. Einstein

Great news! There is genuine, obtainable hope for every child or individual struggling with a learning challenge. Regardless of the particular issues related to reading or other learning tasks, new, innovative techniques based on groundbreaking brain science and other research developments are now available.

In this book, you will receive an education on key issues related to learning difficulties.

Be forewarned: much of what you will learn here might be perceived as going against the grain. But it is by going against the established grain of how one deals with learning disabilities that real, practical progress is being made. I will also explain how parents can find the necessary help to turn their child's frustration and failures with reading and other academic subjects into greatly improved achievement and success—not only in school, but in all of life.

Does all of this sound too good to be true?

If you are a little skeptical, I understand. I know all about the frustrations because for years I struggled with reading. By today's standards, I would have been considered dyslexic.

Because of my own struggle, I have been motivated throughout my career to strengthen weak learning skills and develop learning and reading programs for people with learning disabilities.

And, because of my challenges as a child, I really want to help kids, like a boy we'll call Mike...

Mike is an active third grader who is full of life. He has a toothy grin and is affectionate and inquisitive. He just turned nine and is proud that he now has permission to maneuver through his neighborhood on his new bike—something eight-year-olds aren't allowed to do in his family.

Mike also likes baseball and has a collection of over four hundred baseball cards. He can brief you with an astounding amount of facts and details on his favorite players. He has many friends and often leads the impromptu soccer games on the playground.

In every observable way, Mike seems like any normal, healthy boy his age.

This perception changes, however, when we catch up with Mike inside his third grade classroom. Here he looks stressed: his eyes don't have as much sparkle as when we saw him kicking a soccer ball on the playground. He's doing math and just finished his second problem, whereas almost everyone else in class is about done with the five problems assigned.

Mike looks bored, yet worried. What if his teacher, Mrs. Sullivan, sends home another note to his parents? His mind and eyes wander. He watches first and second graders playing on the playground. Then he notices that his best friend, Jacob, is making faces at Susan, the cutest girl in class. Mike sneaks a glance at Mrs. Sullivan. Oh oh, she's caught his eye, and she looks disgruntled. She doesn't need to say a thing. He's heard before what she'll probably say now, "Mike, stop looking around and finish your work!"

Mrs. Sullivan is a fine teacher, and she truly cares about Mike, but he is trying her patience. While her other third grade students seem driven and apply themselves to the tasks at hand, Mike seems to sit idly, daydreaming or simply choosing not to work. Before the school year started, she read in Mike's file that in second grade he had trouble paying attention and seemed unmotivated. His second grade teacher had written in her end-of-the-year notes—"Needs to be tested for learning disabilities and considered for special education."

Mike's parents are very concerned and find themselves in unfamiliar territory: his sister, Molly, who is three years older, is a star at school, and her teachers love her. So what's going on with Mike? How can two siblings be so different?

He seems so smart. He's almost a walking encyclopedia on baseball after all. Why can't he use that intelligence on his math work at school? After several inconclusive meetings with the principal and counselor, Mike's mom and dad are wondering if he has a personality conflict with Mrs. Sullivan or some sort of a latent learning disability.

Like Molly, Mike knew his ABCs when he was four. At first, reading seemed to come easily for him, but now he is not as excited about reading books before bedtime. Anything that's even remotely connected to schoolwork makes Mike stubborn, angry, and sad. His mom and dad dread the after-dinner homework sessions at the kitchen table. Mike complains about his homework, often crying in frustration, and begs to be allowed to play video games on the computer instead.

Although the family has a modest income, his parents had squeezed some extra cash from the budget and hired a tutor for Mike. Unfortunately, tutoring didn't seem to make a difference in Mike's grades or in his abilities to learn the material at hand the first time, so his parents are questioning the value of trying tutoring again. Mike and his parents are stuck in an all-too-familiar cycle—problems at school, hire a tutor, slight and temporary improvement in grades, and then problems at school once again.

Would it surprise you that over a third of America's school-age children have learning issues similar to Mike's...and the problem is neither a lack of motivation nor improper instruction?

Mike and his fellow "strugglers" are not unintelligent nor are they misfits because of intelligence issues. These kids began their school years excited and eager to learn. What is more, they are capable of doing well in the classroom.

So what's going on here? Why can't someone identify the problem and do something about it?

Good questions.

There is an answer, although it's not considered mainstream.

Tutoring and special education are accepted, mainstream answers. The problem is most of the time they are the wrong solution.

What if, for example, you had a broken leg but your doctor didn't take an x-ray and merely prescribed an antibiotic? Obviously, a broken leg needs to be set and put in a cast. Antibiotics are fine under certain circumstances, but they won't fix a broken leg.

Likewise, when it comes to learning difficulties, the wrong remedy is often applied. So, what is the right treatment? Doesn't an x-ray need to be taken before treating the problem?

One of the major goals of this book is to offer and explain the correct solution to Mike's learning challenges—to take an x-ray and then provide the appropriate treatment.

Before we look at answers, let's examine why today's educational environment in America typically does not know what to do with the "Mikes" of the world...

THE EDUCATION CRISIS

The statement above is true in spite of the fact that the day is coming when today's children will make every major legal, moral, and philosophical decision in our nation. Their ability to sustain our nation's values and way of life depends on the quality of their education, their integrity, and their character development.

This being the case, the successful development of children is and should be the logical goal of public and private education. This logical goal, however, begs the question: "As a nation, are we achieving this goal?"

Tragically, the answer is, "No." The sad truth in America's schools today is that almost 75% of the students moving through elementary, middle, and high school are not able to consistently experience academic success. Even sadder is the fact that many rarely or never experience it.

The National Assessment of Educational Progress (2005)[1], also known as *The Nation's Report Card™*, is a continuing and representative assessment of what America's students know and can do in various subject areas. What does our national grade look like for the "three R's"—reading, writing, and arithmetic? (see figure 1)

First, three-fourths of our high school graduates finish twelfth grade without adequate skills in writing.

Additionally, by the fourth grade, more than two-thirds of the students read below grade level—over one-third of them at or below the second grade reading

THE NATION'S REPORT CARD™

Study by the National Assessment of Educational Progress, also known as *The Nation's Report Card*. It is the only nationally representative and continuing assessment of what America's students know and can do in various subject areas.

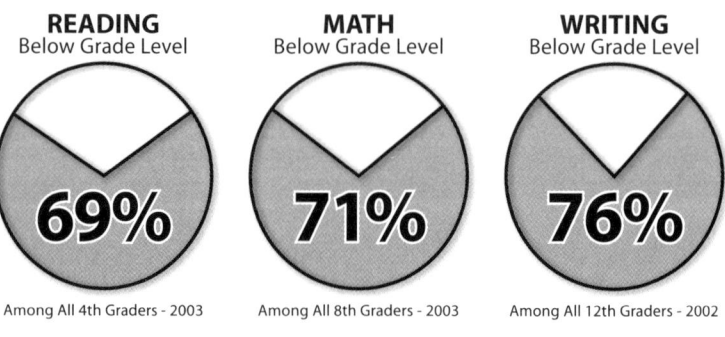

READING	MATH	WRITING
Below Grade Level	Below Grade Level	Below Grade Level
69%	71%	76%
Among All 4th Graders - 2003	Among All 8th Graders - 2003	Among All 12th Graders - 2002

(Figure 1)

level! This score, unfortunately, does not improve: in the eighth grade, more than two-thirds of students are still below grade level in reading.

And what about math? The report is just as bad. By the eighth grade, more than seven out of ten students are performing below acceptable levels.

The reading and learning situation in schools in every state across the United States is in crisis. Evidence for this crisis comes in many forms:

- 85% of all juvenile offenders have reading problems.[2]

- At least 50% of the unemployed are functionally illiterate.[3]

- At least 20 million of the nation's 53 million school-age children are poor readers—about two out of five children.[4]

- If a child is a poor reader at the end of first grade, there is an almost 90% probability that the child will be a poor reader at the end of fourth grade. [5]

- Three-quarters of students who are poor readers in third grade will remain poor readers in high school.[6]

- 60% of the unemployed lack the basic skills for the majority of the hundreds of thousands of vacant high tech jobs.[7]

- Three-quarters of the Fortune 500 companies provide remedial training for their workforce just to get adequate service from their employees.[8]

- Approximately 53% of undergraduates enroll in remedial courses in postsecondary education.[9]

- Of the 29 member nations of the Organization for Economic Co-operation and Development (ODEC), U.S. students are at or near the bottom in mathematics and science knowledge.[10]

- Only 24% of high school seniors are proficient in writing.[11]

- Students in the lowest 25% of achievement are twenty times more likely to drop out of high school than students in the highest 25%.[12]

- 41-44% of all adults at the most basic level of literacy live in poverty, compared with only 4-8% of those in the two highest proficiency levels.[13]

- Expectations on teachers have increased dramatically due to a trend toward mandated non-teaching, planning, and administration duties. Teachers rarely have the time or the resources required for individual, remedial attention.[14]

Parents expect their children to be educated, not simply managed by schools, but parents and home life in today's America also play a role in the education crisis. Students often enter school with fewer practical skills than in generations past because many of today's households require dual incomes to survive in our current economy and to live according to today's standards. Because both parents frequently work outside the home, today's children lack the vital one-on-one learning time that only their parents can provide. Today, children typically spend too much time passively watching television or playing video games—two forms of technology that working parents often rely on for their children's entertainment.

Although what happens at home is crucial, schools still have our nation's children at least seven hours a day, 180 days a year, which represents a tremendous opportunity to influence and impact their destiny. Successfully educating a generation of America's kids depends, for the most part, on helping them get the most out of their time at school.

Parents send their children to school with high academic expectations, unaware that if their children falter, they are likely to be diverted from the mainstream and offered much less than strengthened skills and academic excellence.

Sadly, in addition to suffering from basic learning deficiencies, when children are frustrated and failing at school, they are harmed emotionally, psychologically, socially, and occupationally. In essence, their self-esteem takes a beating, which furthers the suffering on all levels.

America's educational system has fallen on hard times, and all too often the victims of this learning crisis walk through the front door of our homes at the end of each school day. All too often we are left to feel that there is no hope for our children's academic success. In fact, all too often we end up feeling hopeless.

1 : SUMMARY

- There is hope for anyone struggling to overcome a learning difficulty.

- "Learning disabilities" are alarmingly common among American school children.

- Over 70% of students in America's elementary, middle, and high schools experience sub-par academic performance in reading, math, and writing.

- America's teachers are being asked to bear more responsibility—especially among struggling students—than either their time, training, or resources allow.

2 : MISINTERPRETING TEST RESULTS

"We can't solve problems by using the same kind of thinking we used when we created them." — A. Einstein

2

When it's suspected that a child, like Mike, might have a learning disability, a teacher will often request that testing be administered to determine the exact problem. Such testing is not a bad idea, but if the underlying learning sub-skills are not individually considered, the conclusions are often incorrect, rendering the prescribed treatments faulty at best.

During thirty-five years of working with children and seeking to understand their frustrations with reading and learning, I've found there is one indispensable question: "Did the child finally overcome the learning problem?" Sadly, most of the time the answer is, "No."

How a child's learning struggles are dealt with at school will most likely depend on the tests he's given and how the results are interpreted. Incorrect interpretations of test scores will obviously lead to flawed treatment plans. And the child, who is struggling already, will suffer the consequences of misinterpreted test scores and misprescribed treatment plans.

It is extremely important that parents understand the basic problems with standardized testing.

Let me warn you: this perspective on testing may be very different from what you have heard or read before. As you seek to help your child, you may need to change your thinking about learning problems. The information that follows is enlightening and is ultimately a source of great hope for anyone suffering from or dealing with a learning or reading disability.

ACHIEVEMENT TESTS VERSES INTELLIGENCE TESTS

Teachers often encourage administering achievement and intelligence tests to find out what's going on with children struggling in the classroom. Here's a simple definition of what IQ and achievement tests show:

- **Intelligence (IQ) tests** measure cognitive mental skills and basic processing ability.

- **Achievement tests** determine how well a student is doing in academic subjects like arithmetic and social studies. An achievement test measures stored knowledge.

Obviously, achievement and IQ tests measure two different things—everyone agrees on that.

The problems begin with assumptions about the test results, how the results are interpreted, and how they are applied to individual students. For a child to receive help that is both positive and permanent, the test outcomes must be properly understood.

THE PROBLEM WITH THE IQ SCORE

One of the primary issues about interpreting an IQ score is that errors commonly occur in the analysis of IQ tests.

Intelligence tests measure a variety of mental skills, which are lumped together and called "intelligence." The result is an IQ score. This number is supposed to be a measurement of a child's general ability. The problem is that the broad IQ score does not reveal scores for each individual skill. In fact, an average or above average IQ score may result in the misleading assumption that all the underlying mental skills required for good learning or reading are equally high. If the student performs below expectations, it is likely that one or more of the necessary skills are significantly weak, thus signaling a learning struggle but not pinpointing the source of the struggle.

This is why IQ scores tend to either mask or overlook learning problems that deserve deliberate and specific attention.

To further illustrate the problem with IQ scores, here's an analogy: say your car's engine developed a clunking sound, and you took it to the repair shop to be checked. The mechanic performed five diagnostic tests and reported the results as "average"—just the way evaluating skills is done with IQ scores. On four of the tests the engine tested beautifully—a perfect 100%. The fifth score, however, was 0%. If the mechanic told you that the car's overall score was 80%—"better than average... there's nothing to fix"—and gave you the keys, you would not be happy to hear the same old clunking noise in the engine as you drive away.

An average or above average IQ score may result in the misleading assumption that all the underlying mental skills required for good learning or reading are equally high.

The point is, averages can conceal real problems. In the area of IQ scoring, children with an IQ of 120 (100 is considered average) might still have an undetected—potentially limiting—skill problem that could show up at any point during their education.

SMART, BUT A POOR READER?

Many students that seem bright actually struggle with reading. When tested, most of their cognitive skills test high—except for one: phonemic awareness, which is the ability to blend, segment, and manipulate sounds. (see figure 2) Deficiency in this one skill can severely limit both educational success and work performance. (As you'll read later, though, phonemic awareness can be improved to above acceptable levels in less than seven weeks!)

COGNITIVE SKILLS PROFILE™

In this case, the low skill level in phonemic awareness pinpointed during cognitive testing indicates this child would be an extremely poor reader but still have an IQ well above average.

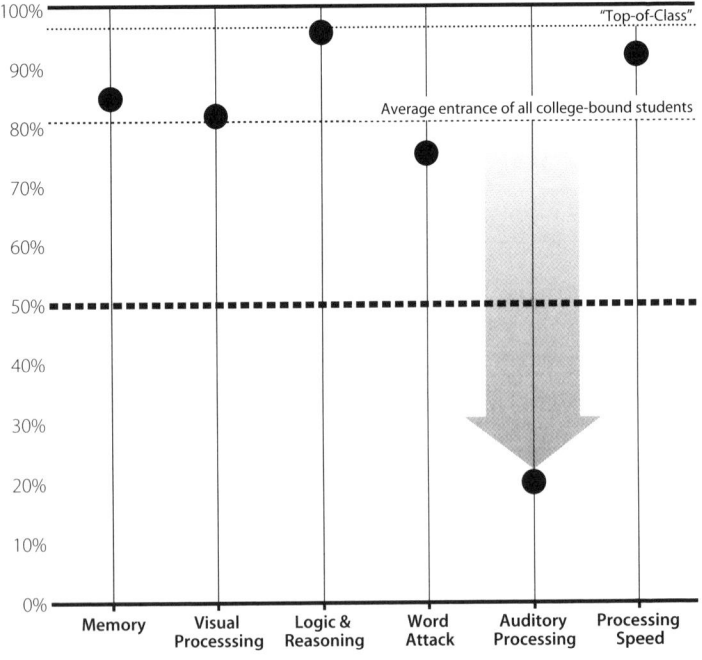

● = Scores by Percentile (where your child rates out of 100)

(Figure 2)

When a student is tested for learning problems, the school's personnel analyze the IQ test results and the achievement test scores to determine if he has a learning disability. The IQ score is compared to actual achievement in school subjects like reading, writing, and math. If there is a discrepancy between those scores (the IQ score being about two years higher than the achievement), the student is labeled as having a learning disability. If both the IQ and achievement scores are low, the student is considered naturally "slow," and in most cases will never receive any special help.

CURRENT RESPONSES TO LEARNING PROBLEMS

When a child is diagnosed with a learning problem today, typically one of five approaches is prescribed. Here is a brief description of each:

Approach 1: Focus on Strengths

School programs often focus on a student's strengths, thereby helping a child who is struggling learn how to compensate for weak skills. Unfortunately, this is the wrong method if eliminating learning problems and helping the child long-term is the objective. With this approach, a skill may be so weak that it can cripple and mask the strengths. Weak learning skills don't disappear by themselves. If it appears that the weak skills have disappeared, it's only because the child has temporarily found ways to compensate with stronger skills.

The tactic of focusing on strengths may appear to work, but eventually time and increased academic demands interfere with the act of compensating, and the skill weaknesses and related limitations will arise to plague the student.

Approach 2: Accommodate for Learning Struggles

A school's special education program is often a good example of an attempt to "accommodate" students' learning challenges. In other words, students are taught to adapt to or live with their learning problems.

Until about fifty years ago, special education was designed to only assist children with sensory, motor, and significant mental disabilities. Then, in the 1960's, learning disabilities were "discovered."[1] Students were given the label of being "learning disabled" because they were falling behind academically. A huge growth in special education was the result.

Many special education programs promote the idea that grouping and labeling such learners puts the blame for below-average progress on something other than the student. This often compels teachers to lower their expectations for students diagnosed with ADD or ADHD. The problem is that teachers haven't been informed that a student's low academic performance is likely only partially the result of ADD or ADHD—that other weak learning skills are almost always present.

Special education programs also typically seek to accommodate struggling students with a primary strategy of lowering expectations to help those children get through school. Kids compare themselves with peers, however, and special education students often suffer eroding self-esteem, which seems to make their learning disabilities all that much more debilitating.

To succeed in school, children need the right learning skills. If those skills are not operating correctly, academic work can become increasingly challenging, and children can be mislabeled. And, when children are mislabeled and put in a special education program, they rarely get the help they really need—strengthening their learning skills.

Approach 3: Tutoring

Tutoring provides extra help with an academic subject area. Often this is the approach parents take when they learn their child is struggling with reading or academics.

In certain instances, tutoring works well: when a child has fallen behind, for example, after moving from school to school or because of an extended illness. Sometimes gaps in a student's academic knowledge have developed for unknown reasons. Extra help can quickly correct the deficit.

Tutoring may help the child keep up in various subjects, but just keeping up effectively means that the student will never get beyond the need for extra help. The child often ends up wearing the "tutoring needed" label throughout his school career.

If weak cognitive skills are the reason a child has fallen behind academically, however, tutoring will most likely just conceal the real problem. As a parent, if you see that your child is not doing better in the subjects being tutored or that tutoring is needed year after year, more than likely, underlying learning skills need strengthening.

Approach 4: Medication

Another approach physicians use to "help" struggling students is prescribing medication.

Nationwide, the number of children being medicated is astounding. At least five million American children annually are receiving a prescription for Attention Deficit Disorder (ADD) or Attention Deficit Hyperactivity Disorder (ADHD).[2] The Drug Enforcement Administration has stated that "...many schools have more methylphenidate [Ritalin] stored on a routine basis than most pharmacies have in stock."[3] Stimulants such as Ritalin and Dexedrine (amphetamines) are the most widely used medications for ADD/ADHD and are often effective in reducing inattention, impulsivity, and hyperactivity, although the success rate of these drugs is hotly debated.

I maintain that the ADD/ADHD diagnosis all too often becomes a convenient way out, not for children, but for frustrated teachers and parents. Children are sitting in classrooms trying to do what they cannot do—read, learn, and master academic subjects; no wonder their attention wanders. When students can't keep up and continually fail, they become inattentive, tend to daydream, and develop bad attitudes. Sometimes they act out and distract other students. Boys in particular become class clowns or troublemakers. They can't sit still or keep from talking. Reading or doing math problems is impossible because certain key cognitive skills are simply deficient.

We must acknowledge that a small percentage of students do have genuine cases of ADD/ADHD; however, the condition is highly over-diagnosed. Parents and educators must share responsibility for an over-reliance on the ADD and ADHD labels. In many cases they simply don't understand that there is an alternative explanation. What's often going on is that a child, discouraged and frustrated because of weak skills, is simply acting out the frustration.

Rather than turning to treatment with drugs, educators, parents, and physicians should seek solutions that eliminate the cause of the child's learning problem.

Approach 5: Attack Weak Skills through Training

As you have seen, the first four approaches for helping a child with a learning disability have significant drawbacks. To ignore the cause of the problem is, in all likelihood, guaranteeing that the problem will never be solved.

This last approach is the only option that does not ignore underlying learning weaknesses, cause parents to lower expectations of their child, or ask a doctor to prescribe medication. Strengthening a child's weak skills is the only option that can bring almost immediate results and have a life-long impact on learning.

An analysis of basic cognitive skills is the first step in obtaining a solution. These are the foundational skills or tools a child uses to learn. Cognitive skills are not the same as the academic subjects taught in school; rather, cognitive skills are the mental tools needed to process and learn what is taught in an academic environment. These skills are also called mental skills, intelligence, learning skills, learning tools, and processing skills. These terms all refer to the same cognitive skills that are needed for consistent success in school, in the workplace, and in all areas of life.

For those students who struggle to learn, there is hope! Cognitive skills can be identified, targeted, and improved. Mental skills can be improved. Abundant evidence from brain research shows that the mind can continue to grow, not just in young children, but well into an individual's later years. I like the sound of that, don't you?

Think back to Mike. More than likely, after testing, he will be classified as having a learning disability and may end up in special education. His homework will be modified and other academic accommodations will lower the standards normally set for children in the classroom.

He may experience some short-lived relief by not facing math problems, but that can't change what life actually requires. How many career limitations, or even job rejections, will he face because of the accommodations set forth in elementary school? What parent would not want to avoid a lifetime of struggle for his or her child?

The weak areas need to be attacked, not avoided. Mike's weak skills can be improved, which will improve his potential in every area of life. His smile and sparkle—a sign of healthy self-esteem and confidence—can return in the classroom setting. Like Mike, all students are able to improve their capabilities. I have seen thousands of students, from all backgrounds and areas of the country, dramatically improve their learning skills.

You may be asking, "Why can't teachers teach underlying learning skills? Isn't that what school is for?" Theoretically, they could, but effective cognitive skill training requires focused attention and immediate feedback in a one-on-one setting. Most teachers have not been given the specific training necessary and, if they have, simply do not have the time or resources to devote that kind of sustained effort to individual students.

Cultural and political factors—plus tight budgets—are also impacting the choices schools can make.

TRUE SOLUTIONS

I want to share the knowledge I have gained about learning and reading struggles; this knowledge is based on the analysis of an enormous amount of recent research on the causes of learning and reading problems. I have also monitored the development of research-based clinical treatments. Over seven hundred learning professionals and fifteen thousand students have partnered with me in the development of programs that either greatly diminish learning problems or, in many cases, eliminate them altogether, thus securing a better future for all involved.

2 : SUMMARY

- IQ scores and academic testing do not reveal underlying learning skill deficiencies.

- The most common approaches to correcting learning problems are not effective.

- Strengthening weak cognitive skills is the best way to permanently solve learning difficulties.

3 : UNDERSTANDING LEARNING DIFFICULTIES

"Education is what remains after one has forgotten everything he learned in school." — A. Einstein

3

The key to solving a persistent learning challenge is to strengthen a person's basic processing or cognitive skill set.

This chapter will answer foundational questions that are of interest to every parent who has a child with a learning disability:

1. What are cognitive skills?
2. How are cognitive skills like learning tools?
3. How do cognitive skills impact performance and success?
4. How can we determine the strength of cognitive skills?
5. Which cognitive skills are most important for success?

The answers to these questions are truly encouraging. If there is an identifiable cause for the learning struggle, and if that cause can be treated successfully, the learning difficulty can be solved! Yes, it's true—learning difficulties can often be permanently overcome.

1. WHAT ARE COGNITIVE SKILLS?

I want to emphasize again that cognitive skills are not at all the same as the subjects taught in the classroom at school. Those are academic skills, which consist of knowledge about different subjects like math, history, and government.

People are often surprised that there's a difference between cognitive and academic skills. Actually, there's a big difference. Cognitive skills are the mental capabilities you need to successfully learn academic subjects. Underlying cognitive skills must function well for you to efficiently and easily read, think, prioritize, understand, plan, remember, and solve problems.

Throughout this book you will encounter several terms that all mean essentially the same thing: cognitive skills, mental skills or tools, underlying skills, learning tools or skills, processing skills, and intelligence. Don't be confused! These terms are synonymous in our vocabulary about learning. For our purposes in this book, please keep in mind that cognitive skills are the individual mental skills we use to learn.

Here are some basic points to remember:

- When cognitive skills are strong, academic learning is fast, easy, efficient, and even fun.

- When cognitive skills are weak, academic learning will be, at best, a struggle.

- Cognitive skills are, therefore, the essential tools for learning.

It will help immensely if you keep these points foremost in your mind as we examine mental skills more closely.

Mental or cognitive skills may seem a bit mysterious because they are not easy to see or recognize by themselves. But, without the underlying cognitive skills, you and I could not process the information received from every possible source—sound, touch, sight, taste, and smell.

When you understand where cognitive skills fit into everyone's learning process, you can see how truly important they are—which leads to another critically important truth: Cognitive skills can change! That's right, cognitive skills, learning skills, underlying skills, learning tools (no matter what they are called) can be improved, strengthened, and enhanced, regardless of a person's age.

No one needs to be stuck forever with the underlying skill levels they have now. There's no reason why you, your child, or someone you care about can't become a better learner.

KEY POINT: It's not how much you know (the information that has been crammed into your head), but how effectively you process the information you have received. Cognitive skills are the processors of this incoming information.

In other words, cognitive skills are the learning skills used to 1) attend to and retain information; 2) process, analyze, and store facts and feelings; and 3) create mental pictures, read words, and understand concepts.

EXPLORING HOW WE LEARN

Learning is primarily a cognitive function. All information we receive must be processed with a variety of cognitive skills. Try this exercise. Refer to the Learning Model to better understand the learning process. (see figure 3)

To begin, as fast as you can, spell your first name out loud...

Let's examine the cognitive skills it took to complete this simple task. To do this, *Input* came as you read or heard the instructions, "Spell your first name out loud." As a part of *Automatic Processing*, you gave *Attention* to the request, held it in your *Working Memory*, and began to *Process* it. You then chose to respond to it. You made the internal, executive *Decision* that this was an easy request; one that you didn't really need to think about, because you already had the answer stored in your *Knowledge Bank*. You drew the appropriate information (the spelling of your name) directly from your *Knowledge Bank* and spoke it as *Output* without hesitation. This enabled you to handle this exercise quickly and easily because it was previously *Known* or familiar information.

Now try this: as fast as you can, spell the last name of the first American President backwards.

Again, *Automatic Processing* enabled you to receive *Input*; you had to read or hear, attend to, process, and remember the request. But this time the answer wasn't automatic—instead, you made the internal, executive *Decision* that something about this request was *New* or unfamiliar. You needed to think about it using one or more of your *Higher Thinking* skills. You had to come up with a plan of action (using *Logic and Reasoning*). Your plan may have been to create a mental image (using *Visual Processing*) of the word "Washington." This may have required you to repeat the name a few times to hear the separate sounds (using *Auditory Processing*) and then retrieve the letter codes (using *Long-Term Memory*) that represent those individual sounds before creating the word image and calling out the letters (as

THE LEARNING MODEL

How we use cognitive skills to learn.

Higher Thinking

Automatic Processing

Attention

Working Memory

Logic & Reasoning

Auditory Processing

Visual Processing

Long-Term Memory

Processing Speed

New

Known

DECISION

Learned Information

Knowledge Bank

Input

Output

Cognitive Skill Efficiency

Academic Performance

(Figure 3)

47

Output). Using all these skills, you laid down an imprint in your *Knowledge Bank*. This imprint would not only help you spell "Washington" backwards, but it would help perform similar tasks faster and easier as well.

This imprinting process can be illustrated by imagining that you had to walk from your house to the mailbox through fresh, deep snow. The first time, the trip would be a challenge in itself and would take extra concentration and effort. The first trip would leave a definite impression. After several similar trips, the path would be so deep and clear that you could walk it while reading your mail, without thinking about where you were going. If you were to do the exercise above (or any mental task) enough times, with enough variety and intensity, the imprint those exercises created would become a solid, permanent mental pathway.

Successful learning requires coordination and cooperation between *Automatic Processing* and *Higher Thinking* cognitive skills. Here's how weakness in any of these mental skills might affect your performance:

- **If Attention is weak** you may have never fully heard the request.

- **If Short-Term Memory is weak** you may have forgotten the request before you responded, maybe needing the request repeated.

- **If Processing Speed is slow** the request may have seemed too complex, requiring the need to have it repeated.

- **If Logic and Reasoning is weak** you may have failed to come up with a solution.

- **If Auditory Processing is weak** you may have been unable to unglue sounds in "Washington."

- **If Long-Term Memory is weak** you may have been unable to remember letters that represent the sounds in "Washington."

- **If Visual Processing is weak** you may have been unable to create a picture of the word in your head.

The point is that if any one of these cognitive skills is weak it will hinder your performance.

2. HOW ARE COGNITIVE SKILLS LIKE POWER TOOLS?

Strong cognitive skills make learning and working easier, faster, and more efficient.

To a large extent, the quality of a child's learning tools determines how he or she will do at school. Have you ever attempted a building project without the right tools? How frustrating and ultimately expensive that can be! It's far easier and more efficient to build a house with electric power tools than with a hammer and screwdriver.

The process of learning is similar. Effective learning is dependent on the efficiency of underlying learning tools.

In the 1980s, scientists began to discover that individuals don't have to settle for the level of cognitive skill efficiency they currently possess. Thinking and learning tools can change and improve. This means anyone can learn and work easier, faster, and more efficiently. Modern science has made it possible to determine how our brain is not functioning properly and how the "glitch" can be corrected. We can literally make our brain run better.

Science has aided our understanding of how the brain functions by doing brain studies using Functional Magnetic Resonance Imaging (fMRI). This high-resolution, soft tissue imaging process allows us to actually watch the brain at work. An fMRI can show changes in blood oxygenation thanks to the magnetic properties of hemoglobin in blood. When the brain is at work, increased blood flow is visible where neurons are actively processing.

Studies utilizing fMRI technology can document active areas in the brain when poor readers and good readers attempt to read. An interesting pattern emerges. Good readers use pathways mostly located in the back of the brain (the occipito-temporal region the area responsible for automatic decoding) with limited activity in front (Broca's area and the parieto-temporal system). Poor readers, however, show under activation in the back of the brain and over activation in the front (the area also used by new readers to analyze letter shapes and unfamiliar words). (see figure 4)

SCIENCE REVEALS BRAIN ACTIVITY WHILE READING

Brain activity differs between good readers and poor readers.

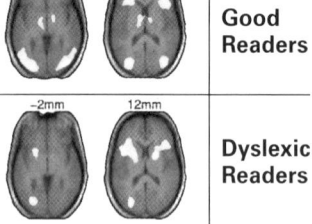

Good Readers

Dyslexic Readers

(Figure 4)

By pinpointing the area of the brain used most heavily while reading, we learn that beginning and poor readers are forced to use slower pathways on virtually every word, while skilled, fluent readers use a more automatic route to see a word and correctly assign pronunciation and meaning.[1] This understanding allows us to measure the effectiveness of various remedial reading strategies. Evidence continues to prove that exposure to intense, effective training in reading can actually create better mental tools for reading. This is shown by the transfer of brain activity from the areas common to poor readers to the more efficient automatic processing centers naturally used by good readers.

Better tools equal better, faster work. Better cognitive skills equal better, easier, faster learning. Better learning leads to greater academic and work success, higher self-esteem, and wider choices and options in life.

3. HOW DO COGNITIVE SKILLS IMPACT PERFORMANCE AND SUCCESS?

Similar to a medical doctor's use of ultrasound or an fMRI, it's possible to "snap a picture" of our underlying cognitive skills. Proper testing allows us to figure out the cause and effect relationships between our learning skills and the academic and work activities they directly impact.

Following are two examples of weak learning (or cognitive) skills:

Example 1:

If a student struggles sounding out and spelling words, he or she almost always has weak auditory processing skills. To sound out and spell words, it is essential to have strong auditory processing skills, which allow one to blend, segment, and analyze sounds.

- **The cause of the problem:** weak blending, segmenting, and sound analysis.

- **The effect of the problem:** poor spelling and reading.

Example 2:

To solve a word math problem, it's essential to picture (visualize) the situation. If a child has difficulty visualizing, he'll likely have problems with math word problems, memory, and comprehension.

- **The cause of the problem:** weak ability to create mental visual images.

- **The effect of the problem:** poor memory, comprehension, and problem solving.

There is a direct connection between specific skills and successful learning. In the above examples, the student can expect to improve his ability to read and spell words after correcting and strengthening the underlying skills of blending, segmenting, and sound analysis. Solving math word problems will be easier after improving visualization skills.

This leads to an obvious fact. If you can identify a child's cognitive skill weakness(es), you can then apply the right answers to correct the underlying problems.

4. HOW CAN WE DETERMINE THE STRENGTH OF COGNITIVE SKILLS?

Thankfully, we have two options for assessing the strength of cognitive skills: observation and testing.

Option 1: Observation

By investing considerable time and effort, a parent or some other observer can list all the activities that are difficult for a child. It is then a relatively straightforward process to determine which underlying skills are critical to successfully complete those activities. Most likely one or more of the mental skills is weak and is therefore the cause of the student's poor performance.

The problem with this kind of observation and analysis is that it might take quite a while (years, in fact) to develop the observation capabilities needed. Furthermore, it requires comprehensive knowledge of cognitive skills and the part each skill plays in academics and other pursuits. Most people don't have adequate knowledge of cognitive skills for such extensive observation. And even with that knowledge, you would still want to test those skills objectively to confirm the accuracy of your observations and evaluations.

To illustrate, think about it this way: even a highly skilled auto mechanic should not depend solely on the symptoms you tell him about, or even what he hears, smells, and sees when you bring your car in for service. Instead, he takes the car into the garage, connects sophisticated diagnostic equipment, and goes through specific tests to see if his first impressions were accurate. It's exactly the same with cognitive skills. Objective testing, instead of relying on observation, is the most reliable way to identify and measure underlying cognitive skill strength.

Option 2: Testing

Properly designed tests directly probe a person's underlying mental skills to see if another's observations and conclusions are accurate. The primary objective of testing is to identify the cause(s) of a limitation in learning and working potential. By doing so, the quality of a student's learning tools can be determined.

As discussed earlier, academic or achievement testing is not the same as cognitive skills testing, and it's important to not confuse the two. The measurement of a child's academic skill level is found through achievement tests, grades, and performance related to peers. Cognitive testing identifies and measures specific levels of underlying skill performance. It does not measure how well you remember the dates of the Civil War. It measures the efficiency of your ability to store and recall the information.

Several testing systems measure cognitive skills. However, beware of any cognitive skills testing that only reports a single score (such as an IQ score). A single score may be an average of up to nine scores, but that is all it is—an average. These single score tests, reported as an IQ, do little to identify and pinpoint the particular strengths and weaknesses that are averaged together to create the score. Because of a lack of specific information, they often mask both the learning skill problem and the possible solutions.

Specific knowledge of individual skills is needed to attack and correct the weaknesses that are specifically hindering learning. The most highly regarded and comprehensive cognitive skills test battery is the Woodcock Johnson III Tests of Cognitive Abilities (WJIII-COG). It identifies and tests a wide range of underlying cognitive skills so that specific causes of learning difficulties can be determined.

The long-term, practical value of such an understanding of a child's cognitive skills is immeasurable. You will finally have answers to the two most important questions that arise when facing a learning difficulty:

> **THE WJIII-COG HAS A NUMBER OF SUBTESTS, EACH MEASURING A DIFFERENT SKILL:**
>
> • Processing Speed
> • Auditory Processing
> • Visual Processing
> • Logic and Reasoning
> • Working Memory
> • Long-Term Memory
> • Attention

1. "Why does this trouble exist?"

2. "What can I do to overcome it?"

The WJIII-COG tests were designed to empower concerned parents and professionals with accurate and understandable measurements of specific cognitive skills. This information, as well as the conclusions of a professional consultation, will clearly reveal the specific options available to successfully overcome the learning challenge rather than to simply manage a student's struggles in the classroom.

The WJIII-COG test is available through

LearningRx Training Centers. Instructions on how to locate a LearningRx Training Center near you are detailed at the end of this book. Our testing fee is normally only a fraction of the fees charges by other professionals because our emphasis is on training skills, not just on testing and diagnosis. You will also receive a personal consultation with a training center professional.

Without question, strong cognitive skills are critically important to successful learning. Let's take a closer look at some of these cognitive and processing skills that help a child perform better in school and throughout life.

---

5. WHICH COGNITIVE SKILLS ARE MOST IMPORTANT FOR SUCCESS?

Since the brain is such a sophisticated organ, learning is a complex process. Many interrelated cognitive skills contribute to academic and occupational success.

Broadly categorized, these critical skills include:
- Attention
- Working Memory
- Processing Speed
- Long-Term Memory
- Visual Processing
- Auditory Processing
- Logic and Reasoning

These skills are interdependent. Often they overlap in their work with other skills, as all the bits of information entering the mind are processed and acted upon.

The detailed list that follows shows how each skill connects to the learning task it enables. The strength or weakness of one skill impacts the general effectiveness of other skills.

Read through this list carefully. You will see how each skill makes a contribution and needs to function well for overall learning to be easy, fast, and successful. You will also realize why the causes of both learning success and learning difficulty are not as much of a mystery as they may seem.

Attention

- Sustained Attention enables you to stay on task for a period of time.

- Selective Attention enables you to stay on task even when a distraction is present.

- Divided Attention allows you to handle two or more tasks at one time.

What to watch for: The inability to stay on task for long periods of time, to ignore distractions, or to multi-task will limit the student's other cognitive skills—which will impact all academic areas.

Working Memory

- Working Memory is the ability to retain information for short periods of time while processing or using it.

What to watch for: Learning suffers if information cannot be retained long enough to handle it properly.

Processing Speed
- Processing Speed is the rate at which the brain handles information.

What to watch for: If processing speed is slow, the information held in working memory may be lost before it can be used, and the student will have to begin again.

Long-Term Memory
- Long-Term Memory is the ability to both store and recall information for later use.

What to watch for: If the ability to store and retrieve information is poor, wrong conclusions and wrong answers will result.

Visual Processing
- Visual Processing is the ability to perceive, analyze, and think in visual images.

- Visual Discrimination is seeing differences in size, color, shape, distance, and the orientation of objects.

- Visualization is creating mental images.

What to watch for: When visual imagery is poor, tasks like math word problems and comprehension, which require seeing the concept/ object in the student's mind, are difficult.

Auditory Processing
- Auditory Processing is the ability to perceive,

analyze, and conceptualize what is heard and is one of the major underlying skills needed to learn to read and spell.

- Auditory Discrimination is hearing differences in sounds, including volume, pitch, duration, and phoneme.

- Phonemic Awareness is the ability to blend sounds to make words, to segment sounds, to break words apart into separate sounds, and to manipulate and analyze sounds to determine the number, sequence, and sounds within a word.

What to watch for: If blending, segmenting, and sound analysis are weak, sounding out words when reading and spelling will be difficult and error-prone.

Logic and Reasoning

- Logic and Reasoning skills are the abilities to reason, prioritize, and plan.

What to watch for: If these skills are not strong, academic activities such as problem solving, math, and comprehension will be difficult.

LEARNING IS COMPLEX BUT NOT MYSTERIOUS

Learning truly is a complex process—perhaps more complicated than you may have realized. But it is not necessarily a mystery. The good news is, with the right information and training, anyone can learn better, faster, and easier. With the correct approach to strengthening cognitive skills, learning challenges can be conquered.

So which learning skill is the most important?
To your child, it is the weak skill—*that* is the skill most likely causing him or her to struggle.

3 : SUMMARY

- Cognitive skills are underlying mental abilities and are not the same as the academic knowledge acquired in the classroom.

- Cognitive skills can change and improve.

- Malfunctioning cognitive skills make learning difficult and frustrating.

- Specific cognitive skills testing is the best way to identify which cognitive skills are the cause of a learning problem and need strengthening.

- With the right information and training, every child can experience learning that is easy, fast, and fun.

4 : THE INCREDIBLE, EVER-CHANGING BRAIN

"Logic will get you from A to B. Imagination will take you everywhere." — A. Einstein

4

Due to improved research techniques and cutting edge technology, it's now possible to understand what's really going on in our brains.

Understanding some of the underlying science of how the brain works and how it can change will help explain why, with training, it's possible to get such remarkable improvements in cognitive skills and how the improvements impact our learning and reading abilities.

Since the 1980s, astounding developments in brain research have better revealed not only how the brain works but also how it can be changed and developed. This revolution in understanding holds many of the keys to the best ways to train learning skills. If your child or someone you care about has a learning difficulty, these discoveries about the brain will give you solid, objective hope: Learning difficulties can be overcome.

I call these scientific breakthroughs in brain research an under-publicized "revolution" because much of this research has not found its way into the mainstream thinking of educators—and particularly those concerned with helping students who have learning difficulties. This may be your first time reading or hearing about many of these findings, too—even if you've been searching for answers to learning difficulties for some time now.

The following Questions and Answers section reveals important information on brain research every parent needs to know.

THE BRAIN AND LEARNING

This exciting information on brain research can be grouped into five broad categories:

1. Brain Functioning
2. Attention
3. Memory
4. Reading
5. Learning

As you read through the following questions and answers, keep in mind how you might use the information to take action and make learning faster and easier. I will share this material through a question and answer format.

BRAIN FUNCTIONING

Q: *Is the structure of the brain permanently fixed at birth?*

A: Interestingly, new evidence confirms that the brain is constantly changing. The brain operates through a complicated arrangement of nerve cells or neurons. Groupings of neurons accomplish specific tasks. Research shows that neighboring neurons are regularly called on when a person must learn a new task. When the task is mastered, the "borrowed" neurons go back to other duties.

"Neuroplasticity" is a relatively new word that defines nerve cells' ability to change and modify their activities in reaction to changes in their environment. Repetition or practice of a task strengthens the neuronal connections and increases the certainty of a more accurate recall of task activities when needed.

As an example, research studies monitoring the brains of violin players by fMRI scans reveal that areas of the brain involved with the left hand (used for fingering) are substantially larger. Thus this part of the brain, the motor cortex, grows to accommodate the demands of learning. Once these skills are mastered and become more automatic, the area of the cortex required is reduced and the brain gears up for new learning tasks. Rather that being locked into a fixed structure, the brain can adapt to each new learning challenge.[1]

Q: *How does the brain deal with expectations and respond to incomplete data?*

A: Input to the brain shapes the way it prepares for subsequent input. It arranges itself physically and chemically to receive more information. Visually, if insufficient information is provided with input, the brain uses its data bank to fill in the blanks.

If you see the left front end of a car in your car's rearview mirror, you assume that a complete car is in the right lane next to you. However, if your brain had insufficient background information, it might fill in the blank inappropriately.

Here's another all-too-common example: being trained to read the "whole word" forces a student to guess an unfamiliar word based on the context of the story and whatever illustrations may provide clues. It's not unusual for young readers to fill in the blank by guessing wrong. That's especially true (and discouraging) for a student with weak cognitive skills.

ATTENTION

Q: *What does attention impact?*

A: Attention gives us several ways to constantly and appropriately monitor our environment. General monitoring allows us to be vigilant. Arousal attention helps us to rapidly get ready to act and prepares us to move. Attention also makes us able to determine the novelty and the potential of a given situation. At the highest level, our attention helps us make decisions.

Attention involves a number of processes including filtering out, balancing multiple perceptions, and assigning emotional importance to these perceptions. These processing decisions are determined by your interest, alertness, and apprehension.

For example, a mother concerned about a sick child will be more alert for changes in the child's breathing than in the sounds of her spouse talking on the phone, her other children playing outside, or the dialogue from a sitcom airing on the television in the next room.

Q: *What is selective attention?*

A: This is the ability to select and focus on what we attend to. With it we block out or shut down input that is unnecessary or should be ignored. This capability keeps our brain from experiencing overload.

Autistic children, for example, do not have this normal capability. To keep from being overloaded, they shut down or shut out input and withdraw from a world that typically offers massive stimulation.

In a similar manner, automobile drivers can focus their visual attention more fully in heavy traffic if they reduce their auditory input (turn off the car radio).

Q: *What is the CEO function in the brain?*

A: The CEO function involves the highest level of attention. It's the planning or decision-making function in our brain that tells us to take action or to react in relation to our goals. It allows you to determine whether what you see, hear, or feel is important and whether to pay attention to it or ignore it.

Q: *What happens in the brain to cause ADHD?*

A: The hyperactive/attention deficit response is the brain's general inability to respond normally to its CEO function. Consequently, it ignores its own advice and decides to engage in activities that are disorderly, inappropriate, and, at times, even illegal. This happens because an individual's inability to sustain attention causes something like an addiction to the present. An ADHD child gets hooked on immediate feedback. For that child, the long-range impact is irrelevant. Therefore, individuals contending with attention problems go for immediate pleasure in spite of the consequences.

MEMORY

Q: *What is working memory?*

A: Working memory operates in the brain's frontal lobe. This system evaluates incoming information and keeps attention moving forward. In working memory, information is held and evaluated, and a decision is made to discard the information or save it for use at some future time.

Working memory is in operation, for example, when adding 77, 89, and 65. After totaling the first column and getting a sum of 21, you need to keep the 2 in your mind to add to the total of the second column. Working memory allows us to work faster by retaining certain information that we'll soon need to reuse instead of taking additional time to write it down or redo a task because we forget something.

One of the major functions of working memory is to prevent useless information from encoding to long-term memory. Unnecessary information can distract our focus from what really matters to us. Our brain's working memory screens out peripheral input, such as horns honking and dogs barking, preventing them from getting into and filling up long-term memory.

Working memory and long-term memory work together to give us the capability to prioritize input. Forgetting can be frustrating, even embarrassing, but, interestingly enough, it's necessary. If it weren't for forgetting, our brains would be jammed with trivia!

Q: *What is long-term memory?*

A: After a decision is made to keep the data, it is forwarded to different parts of the brain and sorted by smell, color, shape, and so forth. Emotion plays an important role in this process: the stronger the feelings caused by the memory, the easier it will be recalled later. Reinforcement by practicing or drilling also strengthens long-term memory.

Q: *Where is memory stored?*

A: Bits and pieces of a single memory are stored in different networks of neurons throughout the brain. The formation and recall of a memory is influenced by mood, surroundings, and the circumstances at the time a memory was formed or retrieved. A memory may be a little different each time we remember it.

Scientists have noted that we add interpretation during the transfer of information between working memory and long-term memory. This means we can be certain that we can't be really certain about our memory.

Q: *Can we make memories stronger?*

A: In a process scientists call "long-term potentiation," memories are encoded and strengthened (and others weakened) each and every time the repetition of a new experience causes neural firing across synapses between nerve cells.

Practice, practice, and more practice makes the bonds between surrounding cells increasingly stronger and gets more neurons involved. The result is a whole network of neurons taking part in remembering the skill, word, or event—regardless of whether we're learning a new language, perfecting our golf game, or learning new math concepts.

Q: *Does memory really get worse with age?*

A: Not necessarily. The adult brain is resilient, adaptable, and ever eager to learn. David Snowden, a professor at the University of Kentucky, has observed this capability in research entitled "The Nuns of Mankato."[2] His studies have included the School Sisters of Notre Dame, a convent in Mankato, Minnesota. The nuns routinely live into their nineties, with many reaching one hundred. Their lives are mentally rigorous and their occupations meaningful.

Supporting Snowden's observations, the PET scans done by other researchers have shown the frontal lobes of twenty-five-year olds and seventy-five-year olds equally illuminated following the same memory tests. This research has shown that intellectually challenging activities stimulate dendrite growth, which adds neural connections in the brain. The brain modifies itself to accommodate learning challenges regardless of age.

READING

Q: *How do dyslexics process letters and words?*

A: Dyslexia simply means trouble with reading. Trouble comes in a wide variety of ways. For instance, some dyslexics have difficulty with certain short consonants (like b and d) while many others have problems distinguishing the vowel sounds. Cognitive training helps them better identify, separate, blend, and analyze the phonemes (sounds) of language more distinctly and accurately.

Researchers indicate that during the first six months of life, when sounds are being hardwired in a baby's brain, nerve cells may clump up in the language center, thereby interfering with the ability to receive and transmit certain messages.[3]

Fortunately, this need not be a permanent condition. Because of the extreme adaptability of the brain, cognitive training can restructure these pathways, removing the logjams to allow messages to flow more smoothly.

Q: *Does the brain actually change as the result of training reading-related cognitive skills?*

A: With the advent of fMRI (a way of looking at what's active in the brain during a task like reading) we can see the change in the brain as a result of specialized training.[4] For example, in a good reader, an area in the occipito-temporal region is most active, and in a poor reader, the activity is scattered in numerous areas. After a period of auditory-based cognitive training, the previously poor fMRI image now shows the pattern of a good reader's fMRI. The brain changed, and we can see it!

LEARNING

Q: *How do parents influence vocabulary and language?*

A: The quality and depth of parental input seems to matter a great deal. Affirmative feedback and the amount of time spent in conversation with children—in particular during their second year—appears to have a major impact on vocabulary and language later.

In research by University of Chicago Psychologist Janellen Huttenlocher,[5] comparisons between professional, working-class, and welfare families, reveal their children heard 2,100, 1,200, and 600 words an hour respectively. Furthermore, positive feedback came an average of thirty times an hour for professionals, fifteen for working-class, and just six times an hour in welfare families.

The quality and quantity of this input is directly correlated with brain development and vocabulary in later years. Some children naturally catch up. Others do not.

Q: *How does practice change the brain?*

A: As mentioned earlier, monitoring the brains of violin players by fMRI reveals areas of the brain involved with the left hand (used for fingering) to be substantially larger. The motor cortex grows to accommodate the demands of learning.

Q: *Why is sleep important for learning?*

A: Apparently, even while we sleep, our brain is at work sorting and storing data in our memory. Research indicates that sleep deliberately interrupted at certain points in the sleep cycle can block learning. A solid night's rest is essential if the brain is to have sufficient and appropriate time to organize and form into lasting memories the information it takes in during waking hours.

Q: *What is the impact of using rewards in training?*

A: It has been conclusively revealed that reinforcement makes the memory bonds stronger because more neurons learn the code. That's why rewards, including praise, are a part of training new skills.

NEW HORIZONS FOR LEARNING

Perhaps the most important encouragement science has provided is that we need not settle for what appears as a limitation or a lifetime disability. The human brain is capable of amazing change and modification. An individual's cognitive skills can be tested for relative strengths and weaknesses; the brain is capable of expanding to accommodate greater cognitive capacity. By training the brain to work faster and more efficiently, learning success can be dramatically improved.

We can set new courses for ourselves, acquire new skills, and set our sights on new horizons with the assurance that our motivation can carry us (and our brains) much farther than we might imagine. We must only be willing to do the work and arm ourselves with the right kind of training tools.

The brain is truly incredible!

4 : SUMMARY

- The brain is capable of growing and changing throughout life.

- Few people naturally function anywhere near their innate upper boundaries of learning capacity.

- Contemporary brain research shows that cognitive skill weaknesses can be identified and overcome—making learning easier.

- Repetition and practice help the brain do a better job of remembering.

- Cognitive skill training can restructure brain pathways to improve reading and other academic learning skills.

- Parents have a tremendous influence over a child's vocabulary and language.

- We can change our brain and our brain's capacity to handle information if we are motivated to grow and learn.

5 : TOOLS AND STEPS FOR OVERCOMING LEARNING DIFFICULTIES

"In the middle of difficulty lies opportunity." — A. Einstein

The overview of exciting insights from brain research only confirms what I mentioned earlier: no child needs to bear the ongoing frustration of a learning difficulty.

We've established that, from birth, the brain is constantly changing—that's neuroplasticity. The brain can be modified in specific ways through the right kind of stimulation. This being the case, the learning difficulties your child faces can be substantially overcome if you choose the right cognitive training.

Let's take a look at some of the powerful training techniques used by LearningRx professionals—a group of very dedicated and caring individuals that I'm honored to be associated with.

NEW ACTIVITIES STRETCH THE BRAIN

When you learn a new task or acquire new knowledge, the memory is assigned to a particular area of the brain. In that space, other brain cells (neurons) are recruited to help process this information. The more you practice or rehearse, the greater the number of neurons involved. The active space in your brain devoted to this new event actually expands to accommodate the assignment.

Application: LearningRx training takes advantage of this fact by packaging its training tasks in a non-academic format. Students are faced with an enjoyable but unfamiliar task to accomplish. They cannot relegate it to some old familiar experience. The result: new connections in the brain are established as soon as the exercises begin.

REPETITION MAKES A SKILL AUTOMATIC

Just like the physical skill of riding a bike, each cognitive skill can eventually become a stored routine. The first step is to bring the skill to a conscious level as your child deliberately thinks about the activity to be trained. As the skill is practiced or rehearsed over days and weeks, the improved skill is then forced naturally to a subconscious level where it will be permanently stored for recall and habitual (or automatic) use. The learner won't have to think about it but will just do it.

For example, in learning how to ride a bike, the more attempts a child makes, the more the brain reinforces the particular skills necessary to stay balanced and in motion. After a short time, a girl or boy doesn't have to stop and think about each part of the procedure to stay upright, balanced, and in motion, or how to stop without falling off. Every time the child rides, the skill is reinforced. Even years later, with no additional riding experience, it's possible for a person to get on a bike and ride because it was so firmly encoded in the brain.

Application: LearningRx training is delivered multiple days each week for at least a three-month period. This creates enough closely associated repetitions to drive the newly strengthened skill into the subconscious, automatic mode.

PROGRESSIVE DRILLS ENHANCE COGNITIVE SKILLS

The brain stays engaged as long as required to handle a task. Drill is the repetition of a single task. Research shows that repetitive drills build stronger pathways and expand the surrounding area of the brain where the task is being recorded. This involves more neurons used for the skill and leads to faster, longer-lasting changes.

Practicing a skill reinforces the mental connections in the brain required to execute it. Repetition communicates the importance you have assigned to the task and consequently, the brain recruits additional cells to record it. The brain's natural capacities adapt quickly and permanently to establish the new activity or skill.

Imagine a basketball star practicing by shooting five hundred free throws every day. With every shot, there is an automatic comparison by the brain to the previous shots. Appropriate adjustments are made in the mind's record of how to shoot free throws. The result: a better free-throw shooter.

Application: LearningRx training is formatted in drills that engage the brain's natural capacity to recruit and construct new connections and to process new tasks and information. The weak functions of the brain being retrained actually begin to expand by recruiting other passive areas. Weakness is definitely turned into strength.

The skills learned in the early levels of training are expanded in the higher levels. The repetition guarantees success and produces rapid, lasting changes. Cognitive skills are not learned like we learn geography. They are developed and strengthened by practice.

"FIRE TOGETHER" MEANS "WIRE TOGETHER"

Neurons involved in the same repeated thoughts and actions develop stronger connections. Regardless of whether the thoughts and actions involve memorizing a spelling list, a musical score, historical facts, football plays, or the intricacies of a figure skating routine, the network of brain cells incorporated into the memory of the skill or activity will be stronger and last longer.

Application: LearningRx training procedures are formatted and grouped to impact closely related cognitive skill groups. The individual underlying skills are repeatedly worked by a variety of techniques and drills.

EXPANDED BRAIN FUNCTION EQUALS ENHANCED PERFORMANCE

If the brain can function better and faster, it will. A healthy brain naturally seeks to operate as efficiently as possible. If you expand brain capacity and connections, the brain will take advantage of the new resources every time it faces a processing task. Since academic performance is dependant on cognitive skill function, increasing the brain's capabilities leads to improved academic performance.

Researchers have been astounded at cases where portions of a patient's brain were damaged or surgically removed following disease or stroke. Yet memories of the skills in the remaining part of the brain remained and could even be improved![1] With deliberate training, these individuals were able to retain or relearn skills in other parts of the brain. These cases show not only that knowledge can be transferred between parts of the brain, but that the remaining parts can be strengthened as well.

Application: LearningRx training primarily concentrates on increasing and strengthening brain function and efficiency. This leaves the secondary activity of academic tutoring to others if such help is still needed to catch up. By focusing on the foundation of a student's capacity to learn, learning is ultimately (and quickly) enhanced for a lifetime.

BIG, FAST CHANGES ARE IMPORTANT

The brain has the potential to expand—and do so quickly. Very few people have maximized their innate learning capacity, which is actually designed to grow. Good training simply takes advantage of these inherent qualities of the brain.

The brain recognizes big change as important change. When facing the call for big, fast changes, people may at first be apprehensive. But, when the big, fast changes happen, they are rewarded with pride and increased motivation. You can call it the "payoff for taking the risk." The bigger the payoff, and the sooner it is realized, the greater a student's willingness to go through the training procedures. Big, fast changes maximize the brain's tendency to adapt to important information. They also maximize the student's motivation and self-esteem.

Application: LearningRx training recognizes the capacity for big, fast changes. The programs are designed to last between three and six short months, not years like some other programs. To accomplish this goal, the training is constructed in a series of small incremental steps that can be attained rapidly. Accomplishing many small goals creates big changes quickly. This approach gives valid, tangible, immediate payback as well as the incentive to keep going. It trains skills and boosts self-esteem at the same time.

LearningRx training pushes the "intensity" envelope and rewards the students with achievable, incremental success. The fun, yet intense training causes the brain to grow, while the student is rewarded and continues to be motivated to change. It all amounts to an incentive to continue to make the investment for the quickest and greatest returns possible.

The training is designed to stimulate motivation. Each time a student completes a series of exercises, he realizes just how much his skills are improving. That positive realization will serve as part of the reward for past efforts, as well as an incentive for future ones. At times, the student may think the training is tough or difficult, but overall growth and improvement will carry him or her through.

FEEDBACK HELPS STRENGTHEN MENTAL SKILLS

The brain attaches value and importance to immediate associations. Connections are stronger between information that is closely and repeatedly associated. Immediate feedback provides these types of close proximity associations.

Application: LearningRx training is designed to facilitate immediate feedback of two types—positive feedback and corrective feedback. In well-designed cognitive training, the one-on-one training relationship between the trainer and student allows for immediate, positive reinforcement. The encouragement provides subtle and effective affirmation for the brain.

This one-on-one design also prevents a student from making false associations. The child is not allowed to practice a procedure incorrectly. Mistakes are pointed out at once. When in error, the learner must begin again, not as punishment, but to re-track the brain's record of how that skill is accomplished and to record it correctly. Furthermore, as training progresses, the student develops the capability of assessing his own performance and self-correcting his errors. It's an essential part of the acquisition and automatic use of the skill.

SEQUENCING IS IMPORTANT

The brain physically changes and expands to accommodate new tasks. It will continue to do this as long as the task requires new connections and recruited neurons. Sequenced tasks do not let the expansion of the brain halt. Capacity is increased at a rapid and continual rate.

Application: LearningRx training is sequenced. Related tasks are grouped to follow one another in logical and progressive steps. This takes full advantage of the brain's capacity to borrow or recruit neurons to handle related tasks. Sequencing is part of good training procedures and brings about confidence and big changes. Effective sequencing includes challenging but achievable small steps of increasing difficulty in the training task. If the task is too hard, the task is frustrating.

If the task is too easy, it's boring.

Training procedures also are designed so the student (and the trainer) can experience a procedure at an increasingly more demanding level and often at a faster rate of speed. The accomplishment is satisfying and serves as incentive for the student to attempt the next, more difficult level (just like a video game).

INTENSITY BUILDS COGNITIVE SKILLS

The brain also associates intensity with importance or value. Intense fear creates indelible memories. Intense grief creates inescapable memories. Physical brain connections are stronger, and priority storage space is assigned to information or tasks associated with high levels of intensity.

Application: LearningRx's one-on-one training is designed to push a student's intensity threshold. However, intensity need not be unpleasant. Intense activities such as sports competitions are great learning situations. As the student progresses upward in capability and ability in cognitive training, the intensity increases in the speed and complexity of the procedures. That challenge serves as an incentive to go for a higher level of accomplishment and reinforces brain pathways created to record the newly acquired task for future use. This is the development of automatic processing (a subconscious habit not requiring conscious effort).

The most effective training is done one-on-one; one trainer and one student. The trainer must be able to immediately assess the student's performance and responses to keep the student on track. The trainer is right across the table, watching every aspect of the procedure and allowing only appropriate or correct responses. No other student-trainer arrangement will provide this essential ingredient and produce such great gains.

DISTRACTIONS AID IN LEARNING SKILLS DEVELOPMENT

Distractions tax the brain's capacity to sort and evaluate the relative importance of incoming information, which involves making thousands of value judgments and assignments each day. The brain's ability to correctly handle distracting information and interruptions is the foundation for focus and good attention skills.

Application: LearningRx training incorporates deliberate distractions as a training tool. As procedures advance, distractions are a carefully added element. A student's ability to keep attention focused on a task, without surrounding activities or distractions becoming a limitation on progress, is important for working efficiently and productively. This skill is important in every one of life's pursuits—in the classroom, at work, in recreation, and so on.

LearningRx cognitive training includes activities that involve the trainer's attempts to take the student's attention away from the assigned task. The trainer actually gets to intentionally pester the student. The subconscious lesson for the student is simply, "I'm not going to allow this to take my mind off of the task I've been assigned." The skill to successfully focus on the assigned task with one part of the mind, while simultaneously being aware that the distraction is still present, is of immense importance in brain training. The student is set up for a satisfying, competitive victory… and the trainer has fun at the same time!

LOADING IS IMPORTANT IN SUCCESSFUL COGNITIVE TRAINING

The brain responds physically to the need to process multiple bits of incoming information. It is designed perfectly to process, associate, evaluate, and store or discard a large quantity of incoming information. Loading involves structuring multiple simultaneous tasks.

Application: LearningRx uses loading principles in every series of sequenced drills. For instance, a student may be required to count by three on beat to the sound of a metronome (counting every other beat) and at the same time listen and respond to the trainer's instructions. Drills like these take a good deal of concentration as well as the ability to successfully divide attention between multiple tasks, to calculate, to create association, and to communicate—all at once.

Exercises such as this will literally force the brain to fire up multiple connections and recruit neurons to handle the task. All this activity leads to lasting, dramatic changes in learning capacity. Loading is a powerful tool used to expand a student's capacity to think quickly and accurately while accomplishing complicated tasks.

A student who masters sequenced tasks involved with loading and distraction has dramatically expanded his or her attention skills and capacity to learn. You can see how these procedures become a valuable measure of feedback as a child's progress is tracked. They are the ultimate evidence of big, fast changes. Progress becomes obvious.

The learning problems a student typically enters training with simply do not allow the kind of simultaneous tasking that LearningRx programs develop. In almost every case, however, a learner rapidly moves through such drills successfully. Confidence and self-esteem soar at this stage. Virtually every student can show improvement in these drills and reap the benefits of increased self-esteem.

EFFECTIVE COGNITIVE TRAINING IS NON-ACADEMIC

At the cognitive level, the brain doesn't distinguish between academic and non-academic tasks, but academic learning relies on and is limited by cognitive function. Academic work means the learning of content-dependent subjects like math, social studies, and science. Such traditional schoolwork requires a mix of sensory and cognitive skills, coupled with memorization, logic, and reasoning. A student becomes frustrated, not challenged, when asked to engage underlying cognitive skills he simply doesn't have.

Brain training is non-academic for two reasons:

First, academic style might turn the student off to the procedures since he has usually experienced a good deal of frustration and failure with academic work. Designing cognitive training procedures that appear like schoolwork would be a formula for failure.

Second, the non-academic nature of the procedures also means the brain training is more like mental games that are fun to play. The likelihood of the student's involvement and success increases dramatically.

A side benefit of the non-academic training style is obvious for the parents who may have spent frustrating hours at the kitchen table with their child unsuccessfully attempting to complete schoolwork. Cognitive training homework (required by the program) will be fun for parents too, especially when added to the experience of observing and participating in their child's growth and development.

Application: LearningRx training is built around non-academic procedures. It's fun and effective. It also avoids the trap of training to a particular subject, grade level, or test. Non-academic cognitive training easily transfers its strength and speed gains to any and all academic subjects the student will face.

WILL POWER AFFECTS BRAIN TRAINING

Changing a person's way of thinking can also alter the structure of the brain. Research by Jeffrey Schwartz at the UCLA School of Medicine[2] found that a person who forcibly changes his behavior could require neurons to be used for more positive functions. This illustrates the importance of choice and self-discipline in overcoming problems with learning.

A student who is not motivated to change, who is satisfied with the status quo no matter how miserable it may be, will not reap the benefits of cognitive training.

Application: LearningRx training procadures are designed to be fun and rewarding. Not every student comes into the program with a high level of enthusiasm, but the "mental game" nature of the procedures and the quick and rewarding successes give every student the best chance to enjoy the training. The entire process is designed to help a child build up the will to succeed.

THIS PROGRAM WORKS!

Every aspect of LearningRx training is designed to work with the brain to achieve success. The non-academic procedures are intense, one-on-one exercises that involve feedback, sequencing, loading, and rewards. They produce big, fast changes in capability that bring the student and trainer satisfaction. They also produce, almost without exception, a big boost for the student's self-esteem.

This training will positively alter mental processing, enhance reading skills and proficiency, and boost the student's ability to successfully deal with academic challenges.

For students who struggle with learning, there is no training approach anywhere that brings the changes in cognitive processing and reading as quickly and effectively as LearningRx's tools and techniques.

The power of a properly formulated cognitive-based training program that achieves big and fast changes can be seen in comparing the duration and results of different approaches to remedial reading. Compared to traditional one-on-one remedial reading programs, cognitive-based programs achieve twice the results in half the time. This means that you get four times the results in the same amount of time. Put another way, it also means that you get the same amount of improvement for one-fourth the investment of time and dollars! (see figure 5)

It is understandable, however, that your primary concern is not with the broad learning needs of all

COGNITIVE SKILLS TRAINING VS. THE COMPETITION

There is no training approach anywhere that brings the changes in cognitive processing and reading as quickly and effectively as LearningRx's tools and techniques. To achieve a 1-year gain in WORD ATTACK skills, each of the following programs will likely require:

Program Type	Total Time Required	Total Cost at Per Session Rate of	
Group Tutoring	**20 MONTHS** 12 SESSIONS PER MONTH	**$9,600** $40/hr.	**$4,800** $20/hr.
One-on-one Tutoring	**12 MONTHS** 12 SESSIONS PER MONTH	**$7,200** $50/hr.	**$4,320** $30/hr.
Specialty Reading Programs	**5.2 MONTHS** 12 SESSIONS PER MONTH	**$6,240** $100/hr.	**$4,368** $70/hr.
Cognitive-based Reading Training (ReadRx)	**1.3 MONTHS** 12 SESSIONS PER MONTH	**$1,560** $100/hr.	**$1,092** $70/hr.

NOTE: The chart on this page illustrates expected gains, time requirements, and cost per program to produce one year of key reading skills gain. Prices are averaged for nationally available services. LearningRx programs are customized for each student; length of training required varies.

(Figure 5)

children. If I were in your shoes, I would want to know, "Will cognitive training help my child?"

That's the important question. Fortunately, there's a simple and affordable answer: have your child's cognitive skills tested.

This is why at LearningRx we provide cognitive skill testing at a fraction of the cost you will find anywhere else. It enables us to help you know, with certainty, if weak cognitive skills are at the root of the learning trouble you want to see your child overcome. If weak cognitive skills are the cause, we can help. If cognitive skills are not weak, you will clearly know that other answers need to be pursued. The affordable testing will give you the information and options necessary to take the right steps to overcome what, if left undiagnosed and uncorrected, could be a lifetime learning disability.

5 : SUMMARY

- The right cognitive training will bring positive improvement to any child with a learning difficulty.

- The brain "stretches" as new learning occurs.

- Knowledge can be transferred and shared among different parts of the brain.

- The brain responds well to big, fast changes.

- A variety of techniques—sequencing, intensity, distractions, loading—helps improve brain efficiency.

- A good cognitive-based training program can achieve four times the results in the same time and for the same investment as with traditional programs.

- A professional cognitive skills training center—like LearningRx—will maximize use of brain research and cutting-edge training practices to provide every child with the opportunity to overcome learning disabilities and enjoy success at school and throughout life.

6 : YOUR CHILD'S BRIGHT FUTURE

"Once we accept our limits, we go beyond them."

— A. Einstein

6

I must say it one more time: regardless of your child's learning challenge, there *is* hope!

Seeing the hope and making it reality, however, are up to you.

I have spent my professional life searching for answers to understand what it takes to help children learn faster and easier. I am so excited about the bright future that awaits children, because we now know so much more about learning problems. But as parents or those who care about others, we have to take responsibility for implementing solutions.

After reading the previous chapters, you now have some basic knowledge about cognitive skills. Unfortunately, just having new knowledge will not end your child's learning struggle. Now you need to apply what you've learned so your child will achieve success. What can you do?

To review briefly, **there are some actions that usually do not work if the underlying problems are weak cognitive skills.** For example, you might try an academic program, such as tutoring, but if that does not bring the results you want, you will seek another method. When you don't see a change in learning skills, you may try still another program.

This cyclic process is what educational experts have experimented with for decades. The problem is that it can take years to see if any approach results in learning progress for a child. While enduring one failure after another, you can imagine what happens to the student and her thoughts about school, teachers, and herself.

I believe there's a better way!

WHERE CAN YOU FIND HELP?

Who should you turn to for assistance if your son or daughter has weak learning skills?

Almost all parents will start their search for solutions at their child's school. It may come as a surprise, but most teachers and school administrators receive very limited traning in spotting and strengthening underlying learning skill weaknesses. Teachers and others at school are sympathetic and want to help, but learning problems confound them almost as much as they do you.

The school may administer tests, but the results will almost always be interpreted in a way that aligns your child with the existing educational model. Your child may receive a learning disability diagnosis and be given tutoring or assigned to special classes. You may hear, "Yes, she has a problem, but she doesn't qualify for special help," or perhaps, "You need to see your doctor about an attention problem."

I repeat—the intentions of educators are good, but because of training, experience, budget limitations, and other factors, they often see problems through the filter of the existing education system.

You must see your child's dilemma from a fresh perspective. No one has the level of interest you do! It's ultimately the parent's responsibility to take charge of their child's educational path. Your child can learn—you must believe this! You should also accept the truth that no one else will shoulder the ultimate responsibility to make sure he or she has the tools needed to achieve learning success.

You may ask, "Why should I have to take charge? I pay plenty of taxes. Isn't it the teacher's job to see that my child succeeds in school? I'm no expert on learning. Why should I have to take this responsibility? Give me a break!"

In a perfect world, you're right—someone else, like a specialist or an educational institution, would step up and give your child the specific help needed. Practically, however, if you don't own this issue, your child could face a long, steep road of frustration and even academic and career failure.

The truth often hurts, but an awareness of this reality gives each of us a chance to respond and change our child's life.

A RATIONALE FOR TAKING CHARGE

There are many compelling reasons why you should take charge of your child's cognitive development. Here are two primary reasons:

First, it makes sense to depend on public or private schools to provide qualified and concerned teachers, a safe environment, and a balanced curriculum. Education systems work hard to insure that the children they serve have these three things.

This environment, as important as it is, does not guarantee that your child will have a successful learning experience. Educators are well intended, but schools simply are not designed to build a child's cognitive skills base.

In other words, if your child is lacking important underlying skills, the reality is that without your intervention, learning struggles are likely to persist for life. Morally and practically then, as a parent, you cannot neglect to take personal responsibility for your child's education.

Yes, you can legally delegate the responsibility for your child's education to a school, public or private. But do you dare do this?

Second, the price you and your family will pay for neglecting to take charge of your child's cognitive learning foundation could be very steep. The emotional, psychological, academic, and future career or occupational costs can be staggering—if you wait for someone else to do the job. (see figure 6)

COGNITIVE SKILLS RANKING AND ITS IMPACT ON COLLEGE SUCCESS AND CAREER EARNINGS

Ranking	College Grads	Avg. Salary (age 30)
Top 5%	82%	$82,900
75-95%	59%	$59,900
25-74%	19%	$44,600
Lowest	3%	$27,700-$11,100

The Bell Curve: Intelligence and Class Structure in American Life.[1]
(Salary estimates adjusted to 2005 dollars.)

(Figure 6)

If your child's learning skills are inadequate, you simply cannot afford to wait for someone else to intervene. Time will work against your child's recovery and progress—lifelong damage could result.

THE LOGICAL PLACE TO BEGIN: YOUR CHILD

You will be pleasantly surprised. It may not take nearly as much time and energy as you might think to make sure your student has the learning skills needed to succeed. Yes, it will require an investment of time, energy, and money, but I want to encourage you. Help is available!

As your knowledge grows regarding what is required to become a strong learner and reader, you will discover that the investment is small compared to the costs of a child's frustration, lost opportunity, and lowered life expectations.

Make the investment to have your child's underlying skills evaluated and then strengthened to sharpen his or her competitive edge. Whether her cognitive skills are weak or strong, they can be dramatically improved—and the change will delight you and your child.

What have you got to lose? Give this approach a try. Take action now!

The First Action Step: Testing

I strongly recommend an initial evaluation. I urge you to have your child's underlying cognitive skills tested. I truly wish that all children, upon entry into their first year of school and then every three years thereafter, would be screened for cognitive and processing skills problems.

If your child's testing reveals some problems, you should place him in an intense, one-on-one cognitive skills training program right away.

THE SECOND ACTION STEP: FIND A COGNITIVE SKILLS TRAINING PROGRAM

Amazingly, current clinical research reveals that strong, basic cognitive skills can be properly trained in as little as one semester! Imagine...an investment of just one semester's training can launch your child into a lifetime of faster, easier, and more reliable learning.

Regardless of which training system you choose, make sure the instruction is intense, targeted, and one-on-one with your child. Participate fully in the training. Follow it closely. Note the results and the changes as you work with your child at home. Is it working? If not, consider another option.

Above all, enjoy watching your child blossom as he or she starts to relish learning and reading and is no longer falling behind in school.

How to Choose a Program or Training

To help you make sure you find the right learning assistance for your child, there are seven questions you should ask when evaluating any training program. The better programs will have "yes" answers to most, if not all, of these important questions.

1. Does the program impact the cause?

The solution must address the reasons for the learning problem, not just the symptoms.

2. Does the program produce big changes?

The payback must be big enough for both you and your child to recognize easily. Otherwise, it will be hard for both of you to stay motivated throughout the training process.

3. Does the program produce quick changes?

Kids (and parents) need immediate rewards or enthusiasm will wane. Desiring immediate payoffs isn't just impatience, but is a powerful tool for overcoming the habitual failure and low motivation of the past.

4. Does the program produce lasting changes?

The stakes are high—you're investing in your child's future success and happiness. Learning improvements that will last a lifetime are the most valuable.

5. Is the program cost-effective?

We all recognize that time, money, and energy are in limited supply and need to be invested wisely. An inexpensive program that doesn't produce results is a waste of money. Another program may cost more but will result in lasting changes. Which option is the best investment? When a child's entire lifetime of success or failure is the issue, the expense of a successful program is a bargain.

6. Does the program have proven results?

Only proven methods are worthy of use in helping overcome a child's learning struggle. Each idea, program, or method you consider should have a documented history of success.

7. Does the program create transfer benefits to other areas of life?
Cognitive skills training should affect many areas of a child's life—not just his academic work. Your child may be treated in only one area, but you should see positive changes in other activities and areas of his learning.

I strongly urge you to ask the above seven questions when considering any program to address your child's learning difficulties. Without satisfactory answers to most or all of the questions, an inadequate program may give your child (and you) false hope and only sustain rather than eliminate the learning crisis—to say nothing of wasting your precious resources. (In Appendix A, the answers for these seven questions for LearningRx programs are provided.)

The Third Action Step: Stay Positive Toward Teachers and the Educational System
When you see dramatic learning progress in your student, resist getting negative toward or harshly judging the teachers and schools that seemed to have failed your child. Remember, no one set out deliberately to label or hurt your son or daughter. Teachers and others at school

are dedicated professionals doing their absolute best—often under stressful circumstances. They'll be pleased, too, as your child becomes a better student. Enlist teachers as allies for your child's educational progress. After the cognitive skills training, your child will be equipped to maximize his public, private, or home school education.

WARNING: DON'T DELAY—NOW'S THE TIME TO ACT!

I implore you not to wait to take charge and act on behalf of your child. Don't let him or her become part of these statistics:

- Nearly four out of ten fourth graders in our country read below basic level [2] and three out of those four will never improve without effective intervention.

- A considerable percentage (26.7%) of high school students identified as having learning disabilities drop out of school prior to graduation.[3] (2005 drop-out rates rose to over 30%)[4] Another 16% of students with learning disabilities exit school for "unknown" reasons without a diploma.

Imagine the consequences for these students and, ultimately, for the nation. These are the same bright children, so full of excitement and confidence, who sang the alphabet song before kindergarten. Now, however, they will almost certainly not fulfill their potential without the appropriate help.

Why does this happen to our most precious resource? The simple answer revolves around the essential fundamentals of learning. Some children's basic reading and learning competencies weren't strengthened early in their education.

What sort of frustration will your child face while he or she is in school? Worse yet, might he or she leave school without a diploma? These are serious matters. No child should be denied the joy of learning because of some correctable but hidden cognitive weakness.

The most important thing is to intervene early enough to make a difference in your child's life. Act now—while the damage can be kept to a minimum. Even if your son or daughter has struggled for years in school, it's not too late to reverse the damage done.

I hate to say this, but even when made aware of the value of early intervention, four out of ten parents wait at least twelve months before they get help for a struggling child. The other parents wait even longer. Sadly, some never seek the needed professional help.

Please ask yourself: "Can my child afford to have me be like the four of ten parents who wait a year or more to try and find out why their child is having such a struggle keeping up with the rest of the class?"

Take charge today! You and your child will never regret it! Remember this: no matter how much money schools throw at special education, new textbooks, enthusiastic teachers, and interactive classrooms, it does not negate the fact that kids have underlying learning issues that are not being solved. Until parents take the proactive steps to remediate and eliminate those problems, children will suffer day after day, year after year. Help your kids become smarter...forever, with powerful, intense, proven training that will alter their academic, social, and home lives forever. You will have a new child—one with increased self-esteem, confidence, and more ability than you ever dreamed possible.

6 : SUMMARY

- There's hope for every child to become a good reader and effective learner.

- Parents must take responsibility for their child's success in overcoming learning challenges.

- A cognitive skills training program needs to be carefully selected.

- The time to act on behalf of your child is now.

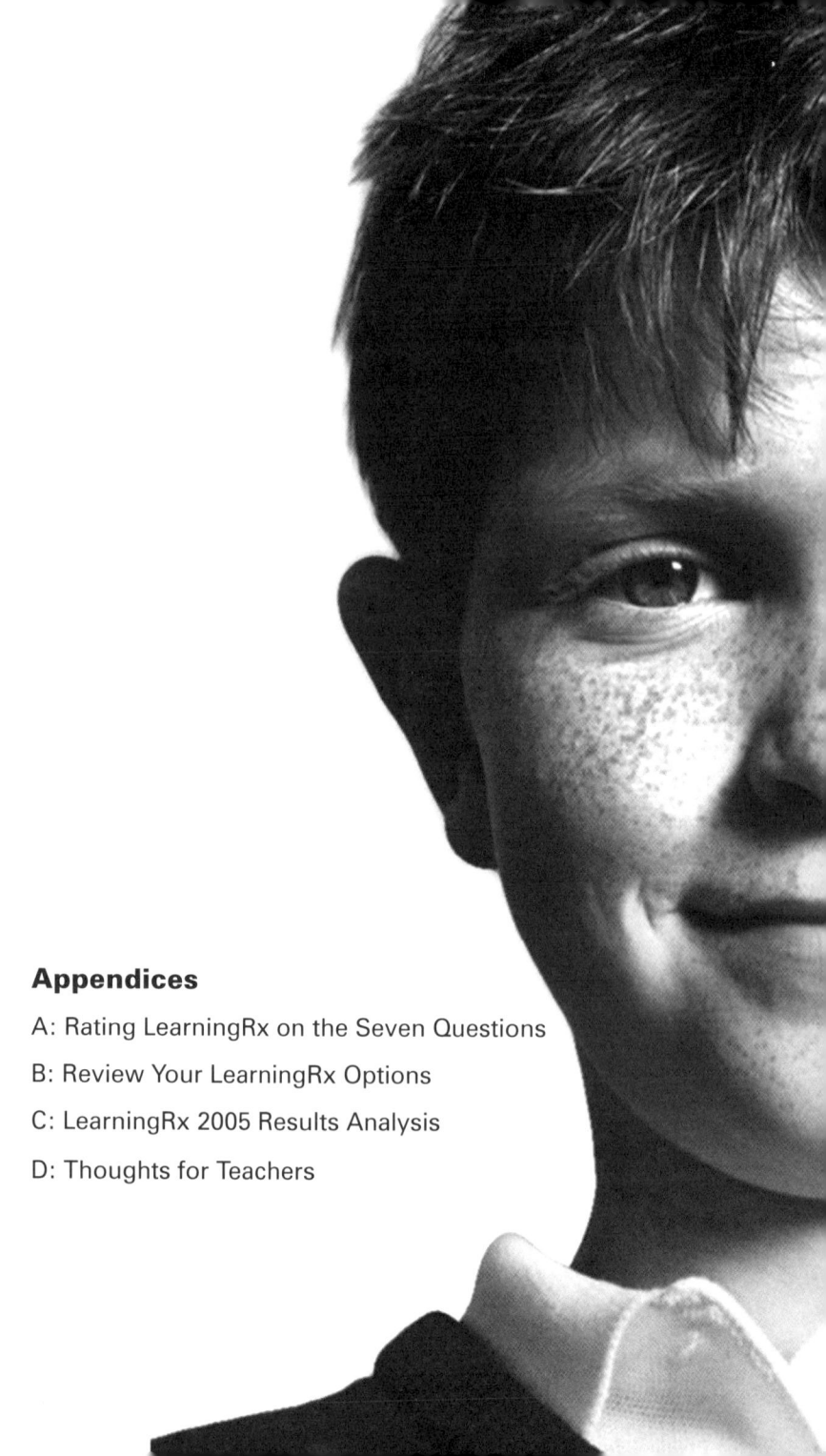

Appendices

APPENDIX A

APPENDIX A

How does LearningRx rate on the seven questions?

1. Does the program impact the cause?

That is what LearningRx is all about. We treat the cause rather than the symptom by first identifying and then training the cognitive skills responsible for the learning or reading problem. Remember, over 80% of all learning problems have one or more deficient cognitive skills as their source.

2. Does the program produce big changes?

LearningRx produces huge changes. Students of all ages, with many different learning challenges, average more than 3.6-year gains in cognitive skills! Gains in reading skills are even greater—exceeding 4 years.

3. Does the program produce quick changes?

LearningRx training produces the above results in only 3 to 6 months. This is unmatched by any other method. Compared to the next best reading program the results are achieved 4 times faster.

4. Does the program produce long-lasting changes?

Unlike academic content that can be forgotten, cognitive skills are retained because they are constantly in use each time we think, read, or solve a problem. In a one-year follow-up study by LearningRx, 98.7% of the skills trained were equal or greater than at the completion of the training.

---

5. Is the program cost-effective?

Since there are very few cognitive training programs to compare to, we'll make this comparison to the many reading programs that publish their results. Compared to the best of the other one-on-one reading programs with similar fees per session, LearningRx gets twice the results in less than half the sessions—leading to four times the value. This cost-effectiveness is also realized when comparing LearningRx's one-on-one reading program to traditional group tutoring. Because LearningRx's gains are about six to eight times greater, the cost per year improvement in reading is about one- half to one-quarter the fees of group tutoring. (See figure 5, Chapter 5)

---

6. Does the program have proven results?

LearningRx's programs have been in development for 20 years in more than 800 professional offices and clinics serving over 15,000 students. The average gain in cognitive skills has increased from 2.9 years to 3.6 years during that time. LearningRx programs are so effective that we make guarantees unmatched by any other known program.

7. Does the program create transfer benefits?

LearningRx has thousands of test and survey documents that show gains in other skills not specifically targeted. These secondary benefits for students include improved self-esteem, faster homework completion, and greater happiness. However, the testimonials of students and parents better answer this question.

Please be sure to read the powerful testimonials of parents and students transformed by Cognitive Skills Training from LearningRx located in the back of the book.

APPENDIX B

APPENDIX B

Review your options at LearningRx

Your local LearningRx Center offers cognitive testing at an affordable fee. With these test results, your LearningRx professional can identify specific underlying skill needs. Your child's unique Cognitive Skill Profile™ will help you accurately see why he or she has difficulty with particular learning tasks.

The Woodcock Johnson III Tests of Cognitive Abilities, Tests of Achievement, and the Gray Oral Reading Tests IV each contain several sub-tests measuring different skills:

1) Processing Speed
2) Auditory Processing
3) Visual Processing
4) Logic & Reasoning
5) Working Memory

6) Long-Term Memory
7) Word Attack
8) Reading Fluidity
9) Comprehension

In addition, at LearningRx you will receive scoring, evaluation, and a professional consultation.

Finally, you will have answers to the two most important questions that arise when facing a learning difficulty:

Why does this trouble exist?
What can I do to overcome it?

The LearningRx testing and customized LearningRx training are designed so that concerned parents can help their child overcome life-long learning struggles. The result: a life of faster, easier learning.

APPENDIX C

APPENDIX C

Editor's Note

An independent analysis of system-wide LearningRx training results for the year 2005 was conducted by the Educational Consulting Group headed by Roxana Marachi, Ph.D., of the Department of Child and Adolescent Development, California State University, Northridge. This appendix contains that report in its entirety.

STATISTICAL ANALYSES OF COGNITIVE CHANGE WITH THE LEARNINGRX TRAINING PROCEDURES

REPORT DATE JUNE 12, 2006

ANALYSES CONDUCTED BY
EDUCATIONAL STATISTICS CONSULTING

ROXANA MARACHI, PH.D.
ASSISTANT PROFESSOR
DEPARTMENT OF CHILD & ADOLESCENT DEVELOPMENT
CALIFORNIA STATE UNIVERSITY, NORTHRIDGE

OVERVIEW, BACKGROUND, AND PROCEDURE DESCRIPTIONS PROVIDED BY LEARNINGRX, INC.

PURPOSE OF CURRENT REPORT

The current report documents preliminary statistical analyses of change in specific cognitive processes and learning for students who have completed the LearningRx cognitive training programs during the 2005 calendar year. Instruments utilized included pre- and post-test Woodcock Johnson Tests of Cognitive Abilities (WJ-III COG) and Achievement (WJ-III ACH) and the Comprehensive Test of Phonological Processing (CTOPP).

OVERVIEW AND BACKGROUND OF LEARNINGRX SYSTEM

The LearningRx training system was developed to train and enhance cognitive learning skills. It is what many refer to as "mental boot camp." The LearningRx training procedures consist of tasks that emphasize auditory or visual processes that require attention and reasoning throughout the training. The processing strategies are learned through inductive rather than deductive inference to ensure greater transfer. In other words, the subject is trained to develop the appropriate strategy to complete the task through the structured experience provided by the training procedures. The training consists of tasks that are organized in a hierarchical manner. Cognitive training uses a synergistic "drill for skill" and meta-cognitive approach to developing cognitive skills. The model is hierarchical and designed to specifically target one or more specific cognitive skills. The tasks repeatedly make demands on one's processing abilities and progressively increase those demands. These tasks are the means of developing cognitive functions. This training approach is based, in part, on the scientific and biological basis that the retraining of cognitive functions can help reorganize and improve higher cognitive functions. To do this, however, the targeted functions must be worked on repeatedly. Therefore, as soon as a student has mastered a task or group of tasks, higher-level tasks that target the same cognitive function must be available.

An important component of the training is the interactive nature of the sessions and *feedback* provided by the trainer to facilitate the learning of the student. The immediate reinforcement and feedback of correct and incorrect responses is designed to enhance the student's learning. This reinforcement is also important for the *sequential* nature of the cognitive procedures. As the procedures move from simple to more complex, the consistent feedback and reinforcement becomes increasingly important to allow the student to achieve mastery of the tasks and move forward to the more challenging levels of tasks. These intense, sequenced tasks and the accompanying feedback are the hallmarks of the LearningRx approach to processing training.

* For additional information about the history and development of the LearningRx cognitive training procedures, please visit **http://www.learningrx.com.**

DESCRIPTIONS OF THE THINKRX, READRX PARTNER, & READRX PRO PROGRAMS

THINKRx PARTNER TRAINING

The ThinkRx Partner training consists of 72 hours of the ThinkRx program for 12 weeks. Certified LearningRx trainers lead three, one-hour sessions each week with the student. Parents whose children are enrolled in the ThinkRx Partner program are also required to spend three hours per week helping their child practice those procedures that are most difficult for him or her. Parents observe and are trained by LearningRx trainers in procedures assigned for home training. The trainers provide constant feedback and sequence the levels worked on by the students. Each of the 24 procedures and over 1000 levels are graded according to difficulty, and tasks became progressively more complex. The pace is regulated by mastery, so the number of tasks completed during training sessions differs from student to student; however, the administration of the procedures is standardized across trainers. While all cognitive skills are addressed, programs are individualized to primarily address and strengthen deficient areas and enhance strengths. Certain modifications may initially be allowed to assist a student with a procedure; however, mastery is quickly established through repetition and drill. Mental activities and distractions are implemented frequently in order to develop complex problem solving and concentration abilities.

An example of a procedure is described as follows:

Attention Arrows: Develops divided, sustained, and selective attention, processing speed, visual sequencing, saccadic fixation, and self-regulation.

Using a metronome and a board with several rows of different colored arrows randomly pointing in the four primary directions, the subject would proceed through the following levels:

Level 1:   Student calls out the color of the arrows without error in 3 rows within a set time (between 10 and 30 seconds).

Level 2:   Student calls out the direction of the arrows without error for three rows within a set time.

Level 3:   Student calls out the color of the arrows in four rows on every other beat (in sync with the metronome set to between 85 bpm and 160 bpm).

Level 4: Student calls out the direction of the arrows as if they were turned a quarter-turn clockwise on every other beat (in sync with the metronome set to between 85 bpm and 160 bpm).

Level 5 Student calls out the color of the "up" and "down" arrows and calls out the direction of the "right" and "left" arrows in 4 rows on every other beat (in sync with the metronome set to between 85 bpm and 160 bpm).

Level 6+ The levels continue to increase in difficulty. Throughout the procedures, the trainer includes a variety of distractions ranging from low-level (walking around the student, coughing, etc.) to high-level distractions (clapping off beat, asking personal questions, etc.)

The procedures require attention, and progression through the levels requires attainment of increasing speed and complexity of processing. Also, as the levels of the task are achieved, the sequenced demands are increased, which makes the task increasingly intense and challenging.

READRx PRO AND READRx PARTNER

The ReadRx Pro training consists of five hours of training per week over 24 weeks by a certified LearningRx trainer with no parental home training involvement. The ReadRx Partner training consists of three one-hour sessions each week with a certified LearningRx trainer and three hours of practice at home each week with the parents. Parents observed and were trained by LearningRx trainers in procedures assigned for home. ReadRx includes the 24 procedures of the ThinkRx program plus an additional 24 lessons of approximately 8 procedures each which focus on auditory processing, basic code, and complex code skills involved in reading rate, accuracy, fluency, comprehension, spelling, and writing. The training method is similar to ThinkRx. An example of parts of a ReadRx procedure is described as follows:

Using a metronome, the trainer says a word (three to five sounds) and the student recites the word, but without one of the sounds, as directed.

Level 4: Drop either the first or the last sound

Level 8: Drop out a sound as directed, varying which consonant sound to drop (Trainer: "cat," beat, "last," beat, Student: "ca," beat, beat, Trainer: "lut," beat, first, beat, Student: "ut,"…)

The present document offers a report of learning gains achieved by students who have completed three of the most commonly used LearningRx cognitive training programs, Think Rx Partner, ReadRx Partner, and ReadRx Pro.

COGNITIVE MEASURES

Prior to and at the end of cognitive training, each student was assessed on up to 11 areas of cognitive processing according to scales on the Woodcock-Johnson III Tests of Cognitive Abilities (WJ-III COG), Woodcock-Johnson III Tests of Achievement (WJ-III ACH), and Comprehensive Test of Phonological Processing (CTOPP) depending on which program the student was enrolled in. These tests have been verified through extensive research as being reliable and valid measures. These measures are considered among school psychologists and mental health professionals as having the strongest psychometric properties in accurately assessing cognitive development. The measures used in the analyses are as follows:

Name of Test	Skill Tested	Test Used
Visual Auditory Learning	Long-Term Memory	WJ-III COG
Spatial Relations	Visual Processing	WJ-III COG
Concept Formation	Logic & Reasoning	WJ-III COG
Numbers Reversed	Short-Term/Working Memory	WJ-III COG
Pair Cancellation	Processing Speed	WJ-III COG
Broad Attention	Attention	WJ-III COG
Word Attack	Decoding	WJ-III ACH
Sound Awareness	Auditory Processing	WJ-III ACH
Segmenting Nonwords	Auditory Processing	CTOPP
Blending Nonwords	Auditory Processing	CTOPP
Auditory Analysis Auditory	Auditory Processing	CTOPP

Long-Term Memory: The ability to recall information that was stored in the past. Long-term memory is important for spelling, recalling facts on tests, and comprehension.

Visual Processing: The ability to perceive, analyze, and think in visual images. This includes visualization, which is the ability to create a picture in your mind. Students who have problems with visual processing may reverse letters or have difficulty following instructions, reading maps, doing word math problems, and comprehending.

Logic and Reasoning: The ability to reason, form concepts, and solve problems using unfamiliar information or novel procedures.

Short-Term Memory/Working Memory: The ability to store and recall amounts of information about the current situation. Students with short-term memory problems may need to look several times at something before copying, have problems following instructions, or need to have information repeated often.

Processing Speed: The ability to perform cognitive tasks quickly; an important skill for complex tasks or tasks that have many steps (i.e. If we are dividing two numbers in our head but processing is slow, we might forget an earlier calculation before we are done and have to start over again. We took longer to do the problem than our ability to remember).

Attention: The ability to stay on task even when distractions are present. Different kinds of attention include sustained attention (staying on task for a period of time), selective attention (focusing on one thing and ignoring distractions), and divided attention (attending to two things at once…often called "multi-tasking").

Decoding: The ability to accurately read written words.

Auditory Processing: The ability to analyze, blend, segment, and synthesize sounds. Auditory processing is a crucial underlying skill for reading and spelling.

DEMOGRAPHICS

SAMPLE CHARACTERISTICS

The original dataset from which the analyses are drawn includes 1,265 students across 31 LearningRx Centers throughout the United States. Student data were compiled at the national headquarters for LearningRx in Colorado Springs, CO. Students' ages range from 4 to 22 with a mean of 11.5 years and standard deviation of 3 years. Ninety percent of the sample falls between the ages of 10 and 18 years of age. Overall, sixty-one percent of the sample is male.

The various programs and numbers of participants are as follows:

LearningRx Program	#	%
ThinkRx Partner	667	52.7
ReadRx Partner	453	35.8
ReadRx Pro	65	5.1
ReadRx Partner/Directed	25	2.0
ReadRx Directed	21	1.7
Lift-Off (Pre-School)	15	1.2
ThinkRx Directed	11	.9
ThinkRx Pro	8	.6
Total	1282	100%

Approximately eighty-eight percent of the sample completed either the ThinkRx Partner or the ReadRx Partner programs, with an additional 5% having completed the ReadRx Pro program. In the interest of clarity of treatment results, data from the other programs listed above are not included in the present analyses. The results below are for the three following groups: students who completed the **ThinkRx Partner Program** (N = 667), students who completed the **ReadRx Partner Program** (N = 453), and those who completed the **ReadRx Pro Program** (N = 65).

The mean age of students in each of these three groups is similar at 11.3 years (SD = 3.1) for the **ThinkRx Partner Program**, 11.7 years (SD = 3) for the **ReadRx Partner Program**, and 11.4 years (SD = 2.8) for the **ReadRx Pro Program**.

Ethnicity	%
White	88%
Black	6%
Hispanic	2%
Other	4%

The ethnic compositions of the students across programs are similar and are indicated below for the full sample in the study.

The gender distributions for each program are indicated below:

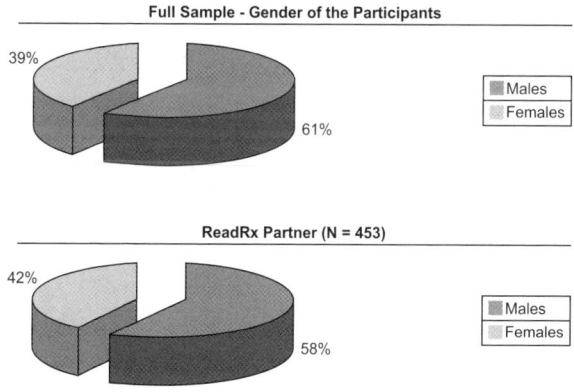

Full Sample - Gender of the Participants

39%

61%

■ Males
▨ Females

ReadRx Partner (N = 453)

42%

58%

■ Males
▨ Females

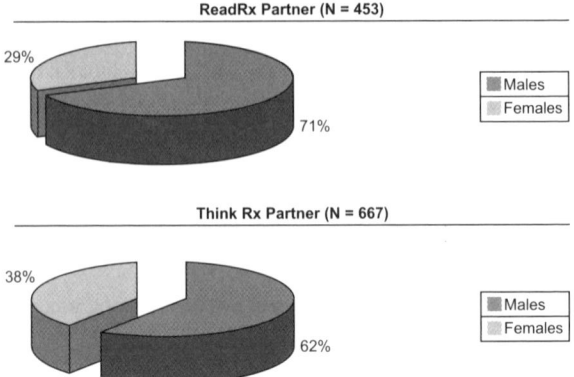

COMBINED PROGRAMS (ALL THINKRX PARTNER, READRX PARTNER, READRX PRO)

T-TEST ANALYSES OF PRE-POST DIFFERENCES ON COGNITIVE MEASURES

In an initial analysis of T-tests of over 30 cognitive skills (measured pre- and post-treatment) every single measure indicated significant increases in test scores after LearningRx training. The following analyses represent the results of pre- post-analysis differences among 9 core cognitive skills that are targeted in the LearningRx cognitive training programs.

Cognitive Test (Skill)	(N)	Ave. PRE-Test Age Equivalency	Ave. POST-Test Age Equivalency	Average GAIN in Years	T-score	p-value <
Visual Auditory Learning (Long-Term Memory)	1013	10.24	13.97	3.73	30.77	.001
Spatial Relations (Visual Processing)	360	12.73	16.72	3.99	13.81	.001
Concept Formation (Logic & Reasoning)	363	11.19	14.66	3.47	20.66	.001
Numbers Reversed (Working Memory)	361	10.31	12.89	2.58	14.21	.001
Pair Cancellation (Processing Speed)	206	10.74	13.47	2.73	16.59	.001
Sound Awareness (Auditory Processing)	346	10.51	15.36	4.83	18.28	.001
Segmenting Nonwords (Auditory Processing)	146	8.22	13.41	5.17	22.90	.001
Blending Nonwords (Auditory Processing)	156	9.31	13.47	4.16	17.72	.001
Auditory Analysis (Auditory Processing)	820	6.40	11.88	5.48	40.62	.001

The above analyses indicate that for each of the cognitive skills measured, significant increases were attained at post-test, indicating a range of 2.58 to 5.48 average years of improvement across the skills. Each of these differences is significant at the .001 level of significance, meaning that such differences would be extremely unlikely (less than 1 in 1000) to have occurred as a "chance" increase. Thus, these results indicate there is strong evidence across all cognitive measures tested to suggest that there are statistically significant gains in cognitive skills following the LearningRx training programs. The extremely high t-scores are further indication that the differences between pre- and post-measures are pronounced. Typical t-values fall within the range of 0 to 1.96 if there are no significant differences between a pre- and post-test measure and above 1.96 if there are significant differences. In the analyses above, the t-scores range between 13.81 and 40.62 and provide further evidence for the strength of the differences between the pre-test and post-test scores.

COMBINED PROGRAMS (STUDENTS WHO PRE-TESTED TWO OR MORE YEARS BELOW AGE EQUIVALENCY)						
Cognitive Test (Skill)	(N)	Ave. PRE-Test Age Equivalency	Ave. POST-Test Age Equivalency	Average GAIN in Years	T-score	p-value <
Visual Auditory Learning (Long-Term Memory)	420	7.84	13.04	5.20	27.8	.001
Spatial Relations (Visual Processing)	95	8.46	14.68	6.22	10.89	.001
Concept Formation (Logic & Reasoning)	116	7.99	12.38	4.39	14.07	.001
Numbers Reversed (Working Memory)	131	8.30	11.56	3.26	11.52	.001
Pair Cancellation (Processing Speed)	44	10.37	14.59	4.22	11.29	.001
Sound Awareness (Auditory Processing)	115	8.80	15.11	6.31	13.69	.001
Segmenting Nonwords (Auditory Processing)	95	7.5	13.55	6.05	24.24	.001
Blending Nonwords (Auditory Processing)	73	8.38	13.80	5.42	19.71	.001
Auditory Analysis (Auditory Processing)	709	6.17	12.03	5.87	41.00	.001

When analyses are conducted on a sub-sample of students who pre-tested at two or more years below grade level, the findings are even more pronounced. T-tests comparing the pre- post-gains among these two subgroups also indicate significant differences in the gains achieved, with lower-performing students demonstrating the most marked gains in cognitive skills. Among this subset of students who pre-tested two or more years below age-equivalency, average years of gain in cognitive skills ranged from 3.26 to 6.31, depending on the cognitive measures tested. An example of one of the most important skill increases related to reading effectiveness is *sound awareness*. On average, a student who pre-tested at an age-equivalency of **8.80 years** attained an age equivalency of **15.11 years** after the 6 months of training. This illustrates an average 6-year gain in Sound Awareness. Other skills critical to reading, such as *Segmenting Nonwords, Blending Nonwords, and Auditory Analysis*, show similar marked gains of between 5 and 6 years of improvement after approximately 6 months of training.

THINKRX PROGRAM (WITHIN 2 YRS BELOW AGE EQUIVALENCY AND 2+ YRS BELOW AGE EQUIVALENCY AT PRE-TEST)

Cognitive Test (Skill)	(N)	Ave. PRE-Test Age Equivalency	Ave. POST-Test Age Equivalency	Average GAIN in Years	T-score	p-value <
Visual Auditory Learning (Long-Term Memory)	86	8.36	12.05	3.69	17.94	.001
2 Yrs or more Below AE	459	7.80	12.96	5.16	28.59	.001
Spatial Relations (Visual Processing)	96	8.99	13.73	4.74	9.34	.001
2 Yrs or more Below AE	106	8.35	14.37	6.02	11.27	.001
Concept Formation (Logic & Reasoning)	104	8.64	12.33	3.69	13.71	.001
2 Yrs or more Below AE	131	7.87	12.17	4.30	14.01	.001
Numbers Reversed (Working Memory)	139	9.16	11.84	2.68	9.08	.001
2 Yrs or more Below AE	147	8.22	11.44	3.22	11.78	.001
Pair Cancellation (Processing Speed)	90	9.50	12.08	2.58	12.12	.001
2 Yrs or more Below AE	47	10.27	14.39	4.12	11.26	.001
Sound Awareness (Auditory Processing)	132	8.41	12.28	3.87	10.73	.001
2 Yrs or more Below AE	128	8.80	15.05	6.25	14.34	.001

☐ Within 2 Yrs Below AE
■ **2 Yrs or more Below AE**

In examining the pre-test to post-test gains for the ThinkRx program, all the cognitive procedures tested yield significant increases in age equivalency after the six months of training. As is evident in the table above, those students with the greatest cognitive disadvantages benefited the most from the training programs. The students who tested at 2 or more years below age equivalency at pre-test had an AVERAGE gain of between 3.22 and 6.25 *age years* of improvement depending on the cognitive test measured.

ReadRx Partner Program
(Within 2 Yrs Below Age Equivalency At Pre-test)

Cognitive Test (Skill)	(N)	Ave. PRE-Test Age Equivalency	Ave. POST-Test Age Equivalency	Average GAIN in Years	T-score	p-value <
Visual Auditory Learning (Long-Term Memory)	104	8.54	12.62	4.08	11.56	.001
Spatial Relations (Visual Processing)	32	9.23	14.28	5.05	5.71	.001
Concept Formation (Logic & Reasoning)	31	9.47	13.44	3.97	7.89	.001
Numbers Reversed (Working Memory)	34	9.44	12.08	2.64	4.99	.001
Sound Awareness (Auditory Processing)	42	8.98	13.31	4.33	6.36	.001
Word Attack (Decoding)	157	8.92	11.36	2.38	13.34	.001

Note: Sample sizes for conducting analyses on the last three cognitive skills (Segmenting Nonwords, Blending Nonwords, and Auditory Analysis) were too small for meaningful analyses (n= 11, 20, and 16, respectively) so these procedures are not included in the table above.

ReadRx Partner Program
(2+ Yrs Below Age Equivalency At Pre-test)

Cognitive Test (Skill)	(N)	Ave. PRE-Test Age Equivalency	Ave. POST-Test Age Equivalency	Average GAIN in Years	T-score	p-value <
Visual Auditory Learning (Long-Term Memory)	163	7.66	12.65	4.99	15.87	.001
Spatial Relations (Visual Processing)	41	8.53	14.67	6.14	6.81	.001
Concept Formation (Logic & Reasoning)	52	7.92	12.48	4.56	8.62	.001
Numbers Reversed (Working Memory)	62	8.30	11.70	3.40	8.50	.001
Pair Cancellation (Processing Speed)	57	8.74	16.05	7.31	11.49	.001
Sound Awareness (Auditory Processing)	210	8.85	12.40	3.55	19.82	.001
Segmenting Nonwords (Auditory Processing)	57	7.20	13.82	6.62	21.77	.001
Blending Nonwords (Auditory Processing)	41	8.17	14.10	5.93	20.95	.001
Auditory Analysis (Auditory Processing)	306	5.97	11.85	5.88	27.32	.001

The two tables above represent t-test analyses for the ReadRx Partner Program and include the cognitive skills processes that are most relevant for reading effectiveness. Consistent with the results of the ThinkRx program, all the cognitive measures tested for ReadRx also resulted in strong significant gains in age equivalency from pre- to post-test. The students who tested at 2 or more years below age equivalency at pre-test had an AVERAGE gain of between 3.22 and 6.25 *years* of improvement depending on the cognitive test measured. To examine one of the measures in detail, we find that the 306 participants in the ReadRx Partner program (all of whom tested at 2+ years below age equivalency at pre-test) attained final post-test scores that indicated an average of 5.88 *years* improvement in their auditory analysis skills. Similar patterns are found for all the other cognitive measures that were assessed. The bar graph presented below illustrates the pre-test to post-test gains on the cognitive measures that were tested.

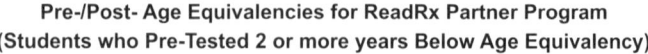

**Pre-/Post- Age Equivalencies for ReadRx Partner Program
(Students who Pre-Tested 2 or more years Below Age Equivalency)**

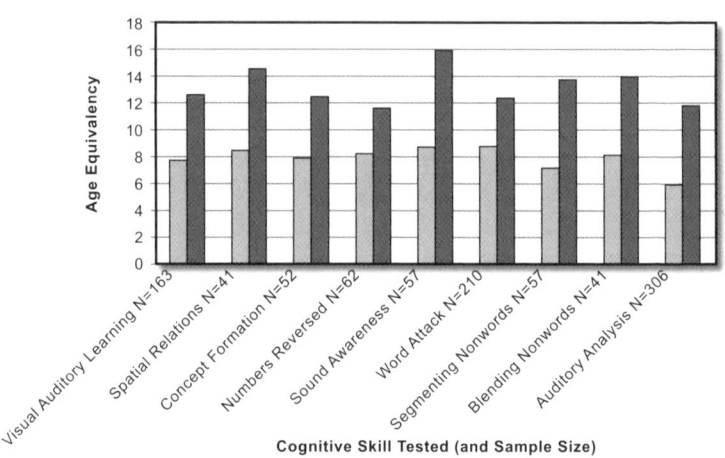

Age equivalency gains for the ReadRx Partner Program are included above. For each of the cognitive skills measures, there were statistically significant gains in age-equivalency that far exceeded what the developmental age equivalency would have been naturally (through 6 months of the child's development during the training). The table below also illustrates the *percentile rank* increases in the pre- and post-test measures for the various cognitive skills.

PRE-/POST- PERCENTILE RANKS FOR READRX PARTNER PROGRAM STUDENTS WHO PRE-TESTED IN THE LOWEST QUARTILE (25%)

Cognitive Test (Skill)	(N)	Ave. PRE-Test Age Equivalency	Ave. POST-Test Age Equivalency	Average GAIN in Years	T-score	p-value <
Visual Auditory (Long-Term Memory)	63	11.32	39.12	27.8%	9.9	.001
Concept Formation (Logic & Reasoning)	44	11.59	42.91	31.32%	9.41	.001
Numbers Reversed (Working Memory)	54	12.41	37.30	24.89%	8.59	.001
Sound Awareness (Auditory Processing)	54	12.43	51.35	38.92%	12.73	.001
Word Attack (Decoding)	41	12.53	36.24	23.72%	9.15	.001
Segmenting Nonwords (Auditory Processing)	47	7.96	58.53	50.57%	17.66	.001

Pre-/Post- Percentile Ranks for ReadRx Partner Program Students in Lowest Quartile (25%) at Pre-test

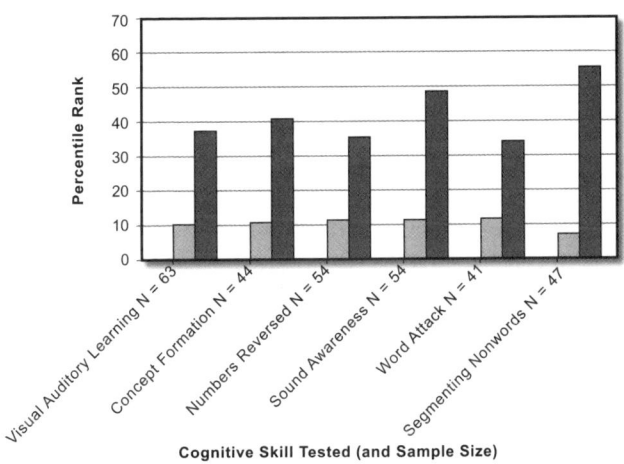

Cognitive Skill Tested (and Sample Size)

As illustrated in the table and graph above, the scores reflect steep gains in both age-equivalency and percentile rank scores of the students from pre-test to post-test assessments. For each of these cognitive skills, the gains demonstrated are far greater than what would be expected by chance. The gains demonstrated above are for students who scored in the lowest quartile (25%) at the initial assessment. These findings, in addition to the ones presented throughout the report, provide strong evidence to suggest that the LearningRx training is related to the gains that have been found.

Pre-/Post- Test Word Attack Age-Equivalency
By # of Read Lessons Completed
(For students Pre-testing 2+ years below Age Equivalency)

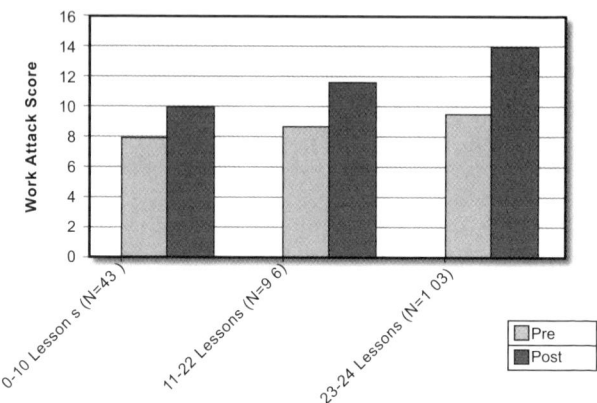

Number of Lessons Completed

This final graph on the previous page illustrates pre-test and post-test age equivalencies for students who were 2 years or more below grade level at the initial assessment. For those students who only completed 0 – 10 ReadRx Lessons, the average gain in Word Attack Skills was **2.03 years** of improvement. For students who completed 11-22 ReadRx Lessons, the average gain in Word Attack Skills was **2.93 years** of improvement. Finally, students who completed 23 or 24 ReadRx Lessons (24 indicates full completion of the program) demonstrated an average of **4.57 years** of improvement in Word Attack Skills. This means that, on average, the students who were the lowest performing (2 years or more *below* age equivalency), who completed the vast majority of the program (95% of the required training), performed far *above* the average age expectancy following the training. The steep gains demonstrated by these students (with increasing strength related to the number of lessons completed) provide additional evidence for the effectiveness of ReadRx Training Programs.

FUTURE DIRECTIONS

The findings presented in the current report provide consistent and strong evidence for the increased cognitive performance of students who have received LearningRx training. Given the relatively large sample sizes of students in the present analyses, the highly reliable and valid measurement tools (the most widely used tests of cognitive skills among educators and psychologists), and the *consistent* results indicating cognitive gains following the LearningRx training, there are compelling reasons to continue research and development of these cognitive training procedures. With the strengths of the results, there are also some important limitations to note that should be kept in mind when interpreting the data and planning further analyses of the program. First, the current report examines data from students who have participated in the program and does not have an equivalent, matched control group for comparison. The present analyses also do not control for demographic variables or specific age groups. In addition, there are many procedures involved in LearningRx training; thus, these analyses do not isolate *which particular* procedures are the ones that could be attributed to the increase in scores. It is possible that the program as a package may provide the best training for students. It is also possible that separate components of the program are more or less effective than others. Further research on the separate procedures would allow more detailed interpretation of the effectiveness of the programs.

As an initial statistical inquiry, the present results provide strong evidence to support further research to be conducted in experimental controlled settings. It would also be valuable to include additional measures to assess the transfer of skills to academic achievement in the educational system. Future data sets should include data from students' test scores on state and national standardized tests, as well as grade-point average data prior to and after the training to further strengthen the research base on the effectiveness of the LearningRx Program. Because of the strong theoretical background and research base that has been the foundation for the development of the LearningRx procedures, in addition to the consistent, pronounced cognitive skill increases that have emerged from this initial set of analyses, it is highly recommended that a full study be conducted and published in the scientific literature on cognitive development and learning.

APPENDIX D

APPENDIX D

Thoughts for teachers

Teachers, thanks for your service to America's students and our future. Your job is becoming increasingly more challenging and more demanding as the information age goes into overdrive. Students simply must be able to learn and read efficiently if they are to succeed in life in the 21st century. You are indispensable to the process, but you are also completely dependent on each student's core cognitive ability to learn to fulfill your mission. This is the area in which cognitive skills testing and training can become powerful tools in your efforts to help struggling students.

LearningRx wants to be your ally as well as a friend to parents as you face the challenges presented by struggling students. We know that ever-greater demands on your classroom and private time, chronically dwindling support from parents, and too frequent second-guessing from the bureaucracy often stand as obstacles to your passion to successfully educate your students. Don't let basic cognitive weaknesses in students make your task even more difficult or impossible. You already know that steps like more homework, time in the computer lab, and Special Education solutions can often only mask persistent learning problems. Cognitive testing and training actually removes the barriers your students are experiencing, and it can do so in weeks, not years.

LearningRx has a variety of materials and programs to explain how cognitive training can help you accomplish your mission, help your school meet the rigorous standards by which it is judged, and help your students learn as fast and easy as they possibly can. We offer special school programs, in-service training, cooperative testing and training partnerships, and private referral programs to get help to individual students who need it.

These services, as well as a group of talented and supportive colleagues with practical expertise in cognitive skills testing and training, are available to you through a local LearningRx center. Go to **www.learningrx.com** to find a center near you and give them a call. When you call, be sure and ask for your free Teacher Resource Kit.

TESTIMONIALS

This is the best time and money I have ever spent. I wish we had found this program 5 years ago when Ivy's learning problems were first recognized. We wasted a lot of time and money on programs that were only band-aids. They didn't address any of the reasons why she wasn't reading or comprehending. Ivy always knew she was smart—smarter than most of the kids in her class, but frustrated that she couldn't produce the work needed to get passing grades. Her brain has been unlocked. She loved the program. She hated the homework, but she loved to show off to friends and neighbors.

— **PAULA BRADLEY,** Greenville, SC (Used with permission)

This program is great. The difference in Joey is night and day. He has even started reading because he wants to. Now that's impressive! When he makes a mistake now, he's always willing to try another way to correct it without guessing. LearningRx has been a true blessing for my son.

— **JOEY,** age 13, Lincoln, NE

I made the A/B honor roll. PARENT: *It used to be such a struggle to get him ready for school. Now he's the first one ready in the morning. LearningRx has done great things for my son.* TRAINER: *Austin has stopped saying he was stupid or, "It's too hard." He no longer feels like he's unable to learn.*

— **AUSTIN,** Tyler, TX

Parker has made tremendous strides in all areas of learning and I truly believe that it is because of LearningRx. I am amazed at how—in such a short period of time—his desire to learn expanded. I would definitely recommend the program to any parent who has concerns that their child is struggling in school or just seems to have to work too hard in any learning skills. Thank you, LearningRx!

— **PARKER,** boy, age 7, Lincoln, NE

Elizabeth had no missing assignments this quarter and her report card had no failing grades. She's off of academic probation, and I see a big difference from last year. She doesn't put off starting assignments, does her homework in study hall, and pays attention to due dates. I don't have to check her work anymore for completeness. Her stress level is down and so is mine. She's on the Academic Challenge team and is developing confidence as she succeeds. She's turning her attention to getting her learner's permit to drive her senior year. Elizabeth is looking forward to playing on the tennis team next fall and is considering which classes she'll take senior year!

— **KAREN DYER,** Bath, OH (Used with permission)

When we began LearningRx, our daughter not only had problems with her schoolwork, but was also having problems with self-image and confidence. She was acting out of character due to the frustration. She was exhausted at the end of each day because she was working so hard but with little results. After only a few sessions, we noticed she had a renewed confidence and was excited to learn and do well. After 10 weeks, not only did we (and her teacher) see a difference, but she saw the difference on her report card. She had increased her grades in all areas. By the end of the sessions and the school year she has brought her grades up to an above-average level. She is happy with herself and sees herself on level with her friends and classmates. She enjoys school and is eager to learn. Thanks for your help!

— **JAMES AND CHRIS W.** (daughter Kayla, age 9) Omaha, NE

My reading level improved from 3.5 to 6. I got a better grade in my science class. PARENT: LearningRx has been a godsend; she has been in special education and other programs since the 3rd grade. Now she is in the 8th grade and it has been determined that she will be in only one modified class.

— **SAVANNAH,** Tyler, TX

Prior to LearningRx, Andrew struggled with visual processing which affected homework organization and the ability to retain things he studied. He'd study and still did poorly because things weren't sticking. His mind was trained to be able to see the things he was missing. Work became easier and he enjoyed it. He was pleased he stuck through and progressed as well as he did. He thought it was cool Mom and Dad couldn't do some of the exercises he could. After LearningRx, organization was easier for Andrew and visual processing increased. Studying is fun because there isn't the frustration there was before. He can concentrate on learning what he needs and he'll retain the info. This shows in increased grades, and he's much happier. LearningRx has been a blessing to him.

— **MRS. BROWN,** Colorado Springs, CO

I am better at reading. Math is not as frustrating. I will never quit because I'm smart. PARENT: Jacob has better focus and concentration. Homework has become easier.

— **JACOB,** Tyler, TX

Halie is a 9-year-old girl who joined us in May. Halie's mom brought her to us in the hopes of improving Halie's spelling and writing skills. Halie improved more than that! With our help, Halie went from Fs on spelling tests to As in one summer! Her processing speed went from the slowest in the class to the 2nd fastest—100 math problems in 5 minutes with only 2 errors! Her ability to write papers has vastly improved and her teacher tells her that she is doing among the best work in the class. Her stories are funny and clear and easy to read. She sits down at her brother's soccer games and writes first drafts of multiple paragraphs in less than 45 minutes. It is almost impossible to distract Halie now. Even when her mother has to come to the classroom, her teacher has to tap her on the shoulder in order to get her to turn away from her work. She now stands out as one of the smartest, quickest kids in the class!

— **HALIE SONNENSCHIEN**, 9 years old, Pleasanton, CA (Reported by LearningRx Pleasanton Center Director)

My son, before training, would do everything he could to get out of doing some of his work...especially reading and writing...because he could not recognize letters or sounds. Since completion of the Lift-Off *program at LearningRx, my son can read and remember things easier, which has boosted his self-confidence. He would not have advanced to 1st grade this year without having completed the* Lift-Off *program.*

— **NAME WITHHELD,** boy, age 7, Lincoln, NE

I am proud to have my last name on homework. PARENT: *His self-confidence has increased dramatically. He has become a much more competitive* Boggle *player.*

— **ROSS,** Tyler, TX

Jacob had many physical and developmental challenges from prenatal brain swelling. His parents insisted that he read 3 pages every evening and he always resisted. Around 4 or 5 weeks into the program his dad told me that the evening before, Jacob read 38 pages of Boxcar Kids *and he had to make him stop and go to bed!*

— **JACOB,** 17 years old, Fayetteville, AR

I can do all my homework every night. I enjoy reading now. I made an 83 on my language test! PARENT: *We have seen great improvement in Ashley's study and memory skills. She works more quickly and accurately. We definitely recommend LearningRx.*

— **ASHLEY,** Tyler, TX

Our Learning Rx experience far surpassed any expectations we had for our son. Before completing the program, he was considered a well-behaved young man that was lazy, unmotivated, and unfocused by his teachers. Although he exhibited signs of high intelligence, our son received as many Ds and Fs as he did As and Bs. Our son found a LearningRx brochure in the trash can and essentially begged for help as the anecdotes in the flyer sounded like his own personal story. As he began training with Mrs. Gloria, things started changing immediately. Our son stated that for the first time he actually felt he had partners (Mrs. Gloria and Mrs. Diane) that were on his side to support him in every way. We are especially grateful for the patience and support that Mrs. Gloria provided each time she worked with him. Her encouragement led him to take ownership of his training and thus he studied tirelessly at home in order to meet his goal at completing the program successfully. As a result, our son received all As on his last report card (with the exception of one B, where he scored an 89.4%), made All Region Band, and received 4th place in the Regional Geometry contest at UALR.

— **KW** (Mother of a 15-year-old son) Little Rock, AR

A 13-year-old boy who was diagnosed with ADD came to us for help. He was having trouble reading, remembering and comprehending. His parents had to fight with him to even pick up a book. Halfway through the program, he came into his parents' bedroom at 12:30 am simply to tell them about the book he was reading. He now discusses Harry Potter *with his friends and competes with them to finish new books. His long-term memory improved by 11 years! His auditory working memory went up 22 years! He was able to reduce his strength of ADD medication in school and is extremely happy about it. His mother refers to him as the new version of himself!*

— **NAME WITHHELD,** 9 years old, Pleasanton, CA
(Reported by LearningRx Pleasanton Center Director)

I brought my English grade up from 72 to 95 in three weeks. I feel like I have progressed in reading and writing. PARENT: *The sooner you enroll your child, the sooner you will see the benefits.*

— **MONICA,** Tyler, TX

My son has shown tremendous gains in his ability to read and to do his homework on his own. He has much more confidence in himself and his abilities. He doesn't have to be told over and over to do simple things such as brush your teeth, take a bath, and get in the bed. He functions on his own so much better at home and at school. His teachers have all commented they don't have to constantly remind him what to do such as getting books, paper, and a pencil ready for the next task.

This program has brought him up to grade level and has given us the tools and knowledge of how to continue on with him so he can become a normal functioning adult.

Thank you all so much!

— **SC** (Mother of a 10-year-old son) Little Rock, AR

We would (and do) enthusiastically recommend your programs. In the beginning, we noticed small things, like Daniel enjoyed playing cards (UNO and Go Fish) and other games more without becoming so frustrated. We also pretty quickly saw his self-esteem increase. The love and affirmation he received from [his trainer] and the successes he was experiencing in his training really made him feel good about himself.

His attention span has definitely improved along with his ability to concentrate.

His reading has improved dramatically. He is much more confident of his ability, so he is willing to push himself to read more difficult books. His math has also improved. He moves much more quickly through his work and does his work more independently.

Daniel has also just loved coming to see everyone—from the LearningRx Director and Staff, to the other trainers and students. He has felt like LearningRx is a fun, safe, loving place, which has helped get him to each session—because it has been fun work—for him and us!

Thanks so much for everything. Cassandra has been beyond wonderful. We believe the Lord truly placed us together at this particular time in Daniel's life. What a blessing you all have been.

— **DANIEL SMITH,** (Mom: Deborah) Greenville, SC

Before my son began LearningRx, he was struggling greatly in school with staying focused and beginning and finishing his work. He was on medication for ADHD and depression. In just a few weeks he was off the anti-depressant and had become a lot more sociable and confident in himself. For about two years prior to beginning LearningRx he spent his spare time at home alone. This summer he was at the pool daily, he rode his bike more than ever, was spending the night with other friends, and having them spend the night with him. He easily made friends in new places when before he would have refused to go to new places. He did not take one pill for ADHD the entire summer and I still have all of my hair. His therapists/psychiatrists are very excited about the improvements he had made due to LearningRx and are looking forward to learning more about the program so they can recommend LearningRx to their patients.

My son began LearningRx just a few weeks before the end of the school year so we have not had a chance to see how well it will help with schoolwork. But, we are confident that once he starts school this week, the changes we will see will be phenomenal! His day-to-day tasks show us that he is more alert to what is going on around him. When he thinks he has forgotten something we have told him, he is amazed to find that if he thinks for a minute, he remembers. When told to do something, he will usually do it right away, without as much argument as before, if he argues at all. He can go into his room to clean it and not feel overwhelmed. He can go in and assess the situation and begin on his own and can continue cleaning and organizing on his own. Those are the things he could not do before. These things show me that when school starts he will be able to work more independently, begin working on his own without being pushed, be able to keep up with note taking, and when taking tests, be able to remember the answers.

My son will be starting a new school this week, he is not anxious about it. He is actually getting excited *about it. Two years ago, he was so anxious about school that even two months into school he would get sick in the morning. This was a school where he had schoolmates he had known for two years. The school he will begin this week, he will not know anyone.*

I am so looking forward to this school year. I believe that there will be a lot less stress than the past three years have been. LearningRx is the reason for this. I would highly recommend it to anyone, child or adult. This program would be beneficial to anyone. I have two more children, one with ADHD and one without. I plan for both of them to eventually be students at LearningRx. My husband runs a company that employs people who have to be able to put a lot of detail into their work. He is looking at LearningRx to offer training for employees.

The investment may seem like a lot, but I can tell you it's worth it. If all my son was to get out of this was confidence in himself and greater self-esteem it would be worth it. Seeing the smile on his face and hearing him laugh was worth every penny.

When we received our post-test scores, we knew that there would be a great improvement, but what we saw on paper was amazing. It was more than we expected. His age equivalence jumped anywhere from 2.5 years to 11.5 years. It was amazing.

— **ES,** 14 years old, Little Rock, AR

Our daughter was struggling in middle school academically; primarily in not reaching her potential in all subjects. Because her grades and scores were not to our satisfaction, we went through numerous teacher conferences, positive and negative reinforcement discipline techniques, filled out multiple ADHD score sheets, talked to friends, teachers, church teachers, family members, and other parents to see what we as parents had done or were doing wrong.

We tried tutoring and taking away extracurricular activities and finally had a formal evaluation with two Ph.D. private school psychologists. We were able to see that our daughter had a learning style that was weak with auditory input and strongest with oral and visual input. She learned best with creative presentations of routine material.

The solution was to tutor for her learning style but that wasn't effective and we had resorted to repeating her years until we heard of LearningRx. LearningRx can best describe its strengths and methods in its own literature that is readily available. Our experience after 18 weeks is that LearningRx was able to quickly assess and pinpoint our daughter's learning style and quickly correct it through diligent and consistent brain training exercises and assignments. The staff was indispensable and the training was great. Her improvement has been in all areas and has been notably improved across all measurable points. She now has a foundation to build on, will continue the exercises, and will hopefully finish her year strong with grades that she has always been capable of.

— **Elizabeth Eberly,** 13 years old, (Dad: Dr. John Eberly, M.D.) Greenville, SC

REFERENCES & ADDTIONAL READING

REFERENCES & ADDTIONAL READING

Chapter 1

1 Perie, M., Grigg, W., and Donahue, P. *The Nation's Report Card: Reading 2005* (NCES 2006-451). U.S. Department of Education, National Center for Education Statistics. Washington, DC: U.S. Government Printing Office. 2005.

2 Hock, M. and Deshler, D. *Don't Forget the Adolescents.* The University of Kansas Center for Research on Learning. Principal Leadership. 2003.

3 McEntyre, Marilyn. *Why Worry About Words?* Westmont College: 2004 Stone Lectures (October 4, 2004). Theology Today ISSN 0040-5736.

4 Henry, Tamara. *Lawmakers move to improve literacy.* USA Today: Nation. June 20, 2001.

5 Boyer, Ernest L. *Ready to learn: A mandate for the nation.* Report by Carnegie Foundation for the Advancement of Teaching. Princeton, NJ: The Carnegie Foundation for the Advancement of Teaching. 1991.

6 Shaywitz, MD, Sally, et al. *Predicting Reading Performance form Neuroimaging Profiles: The Cerebral Basis of Phonological Effects in Printed Word Identification.* Journal of Experimental Psychology: Human Perception and Performance. Volume 23, Number 2 (299-318). 1997.

7 Ohio Literacy Research Center: Adult Literacy: The Foundation for Progress-Employment, November 2005. http://literacy.kent.edu/Oasis/Resc/Educ/fb2.html

8 Lartigue, Casey. *Why Not Sue 'Big Schooling?'* Oklahoma Council for Public Affairs. Volume 9, Number 12. December 2002.

9 Adolescent Literacy Policy Update. Alliance for Excellent Education. Issue Brief, June 2005. http://www.all4ed.org/publications/ReadingNext/AdolescentLiteracyFactSheet.pdf

10 *America's Pressing Challenge: Building a Stronger Foundation.* National Science Board (NSB): A Companion to Science and Engineering Indicators. 06-02. January 2006.

11 U.S. Department of Education, Institute of Education Sciences, National Center for Education Statistics, National Assessment of Educational Progress (NAEP). 1998 and 2002 Writing Assessments.

12 Carnevale, A. *Help wanted...college required.* Leadership 2000 Series. Princeton, NJ: Educational Testing Service. 2001.

13 Kirsch, I., Jungeblut, A., Jenkins, L., and Kolstad, A. *1992 Adult Literacy Products—Executive Summary of Adult Literacy in America: A First Look at the Results of the National Adult Literacy Survey.* National Assessment of Adult Literacy (NAAL). 1992.

14 Committee to Study Teacher Workload, Planning Time, and Assessments. *Joint Taskforce on Workload, Planning, and Assessments (HCEA).* June 2003. http://hceanea.org/Committee_Report_to_BOE_June_26_2003.pdf

Chapter 2

1   Kirk, Samuel. *Behavioral Diagnosis and Remediation of Learning Disabilities.* Proceedings on the conference into the problems of the perceptually handicapped child. 1st Annual, Chicago, Illinois. Volume 1. April 6, 1963.

2   LeFever, G., Arcona, A., and Antonuccio, D. *ADHD Among American Schoolchildren: Evidence of Overdiagnosis and Overuse of Medication.* The Scientific Review of Mental Health Practice. Volume 2, Number 1. Spring/Summer 2003.

3   Woodworth, Terrance. Deputy Director—Office of Diversion Control—Drug Enforcement Administration. DEA Congressional Testimony Committee on Education and the Workforce: Subcommittee on Early Childhood, Youth, and Families. May 16, 2000.

Chapter 3

1   Shaywitz, MD, S. *Overcoming Dyslexia: A New and Complete Science-Based Program for Reading Problems at Any Level.* Vintage Books. 2005.

Chapter 4

1   Ratey, MD, J. *A User's Guide to the Brain: Perception, Attention, and the Four Theaters of the Brain.* Pantheon Books. 2001.

2   Snowdon, David. *Aging with Grace: What the Nun Study Teaches Us About Leading Longer, Healthier, and More Meaningful Lives.* Bantam Books. 2001.

3   Gopnik, A., Meltzoff, A., and Kuhl, P. *The Scientist in the Crib: Minds, Brains, and How Children Learn.* William Morrow & Company. 1999.

4   Karnia, A. Karnia., Morocza, I.A., Bitana, T., Shaule, S., Kushnirb,

T., Breznitz, Z. *An fMRI study of the differential effects of word presentation rates (reading acceleration) on dyslexic readers' brain activity patterns.* Journal of Neurolinguistics. 18 (197–219). 2005.

5   Huttenlocher, J., et al. *Early Vocabulary Growth: Relation to Language Input andGender.* Developmental Psychology (27). 1991.

Chapter 5

1   Ratey, MD, J. *A User's Guide to the Brain: Perception, Attention, and the Four Theaters of the Brain.* Pantheon Books. 2001.

2   Schwartz, J. and Begley, S. *The Mind and the Brain: Neuroplasticity and the Power of Mental Force.* Regan Books. 2002.

Chapter 6

1   Hernstein, R. and Murray, C. *The Bell Curve: Intelligence and Class Structure in American Life.* The Free Press. 1994.

2   Perie, M., Grigg, W., and Donahue, P. *The Nation's Report Card: Reading 2005* (NCES 2006-451). U.S. Department of Education, National Center for Education Statistics. Washington, DC: U.S. Government Printing Office. 2005.

3   G. Reid Lyon, *Special Education for Students with Disabilities; The Future of Children.* Volume 6 - Number 1 – 1996

4   Thornburgh, Nathan. *Dropout Nation.* TIME. April 17, 2006.

Additional Reading

Bracken, Bruce. *Special Issue Intelligence: Theories and Practice.* Journal of Psychoeducation Assessment. Volume 8, Number 3. The Psychoeducational Corporation. 1990.

Feuerstein, Reuven. *Don't Accept Me as I am: Helping "Retarded" People to Excel.* Plenum Press. 1988.

Feuerstein, Reuven. *Instrumental Enrichment.* University Park Press. 1980.

Gardner, Howard. *Frames of Mind.* Basic Books. 1983.

Gardner, Richard. *The Objective Diagnosis of Minimal Brain Dysfunction. Creative Therapeutics.* 1979.

Gopnik, A., Meltzoff, A., and Kuhl, P. *The Scientist in the Crib: Minds, Brains, and How Children Learn.* William Morrow & Company. 1999.

Herrmann, Douglas. *Improving Student Memory.* Hogrefe and Huber. 1993.

Herrnstein, R. and Murray, C. *The Bell Curve: Intelligence and Class Structure in American Life.* The Free Press. 1994.

Kirby, J. and Williams, N. *Learning Problems: A Cognitive Approach.* Kagan and Woo Limited. 1991.

Kirk, Samuel. *The Development and Psychometric Characteristics of the Revised Illinois Test of Psycholinguistic Abilities.* University of Illinois Press. 1969.

Lorayne, H. and Lucas, J. *The Memory Book.* Ballantine Books. 1974.

Lyon, G. Reid. *Frames of Reference for the Assessment of Learning Disabilities.* Paul H. Brookes Publishing. 1993.

Maddox, Harry. *How to Study.* Ballantine Books. 1963.

McGuinness, Ph.D., Diane. *Why Our Children Can't Read and What We Can Do About It.* A Touchstone Book. 1997.

Orem, R.C. *Learning to See.* Mafex Associates. 1965.

Parasuraman, Raja. *Varieties of Attention.* Academic Press. 1984.

Ratey, M.D., John. *User's Guide to the Brain: Perception, Attention, and the Four Theaters of the Brain.* Pantheon Books. 2001.

Salny, Abbie. *The Mensa Think-Smart Book.* Harper & Row. 1986.

Scheiman, Mitchell. *Optometric Management of Learning-Related Vision Problems.* Mosby. 1994.

Schwartz, J. and Begley, S. *The Mind and the Brain: Neuroplasticity and the Power of Mental Force.* Regan Books. 2002.

Shaywitz, M.D., S. *Overcoming Dyslexia: A New and Complete Science-Based Program for Reading Problems at Any Level.* Vintage Books. 2005.

Snowdon, David. *Aging with Grace: What the Nun Study Teaches Us About Leading Longer, Healthier, and More Meaningful Lives.* Bantam Books. 2001.

Solan, Harold. *Developmental and Perceptual Assessment of Learning-Disabled Children.* Optometric Extension Program (OEP). 1994.

Sommer, Robert. *The Mind's Eye.* Dale Seymour Publications. 1978.

Sternberg, R. and Detterman, D. *How and How Much Can Intelligence Be Increased?* Ablex Publishing. 1982.

Sternberg, R. and Detterman, D. *What is Intelligence?* Ablex Publishing. 1986.

Van Witsen, Betty. *Perceptual Training Activities Handbook.* Teachers College Press. 1958.

Vernon, Philip. *Speed of Information-Processing and Intelligence.* Ablex Publishing. 1987.

Vos Savant, Marilyn. *Brain Building: Exercising Yourself Smarter.* Bantam Books. 1990.

NOTES

NOTES

RESOURCES

TO CONTACT A LEARNINGRX CENTER NEAR YOU

LearningRx, Inc. is a network of cognitive skill and reading training professionals who are actively engaged in enhancing the learning ability of students all across the nation. Visit **www.learningrx.com** to locate a center near you, and call today.

ONLINE RESOURCES FROM LEARNINGRx

Once you log on to **www.learningrx.com**, you can also:

- Take a free skills Self-Screening
- Learn about the founder of LearningRx, Dr. Ken Gibson
- Discover the history and development of the LearningRx programs
- Learn more about cognitive-based learning and reading training
- Explore the science behind cognitive skills testing and training
- Download a free special report entitled "Overcoming Learning Disabilities"
- Sign up for a complimentary subscription to *LearningRx Magazine*

IF THERE IS NOT A LEARNINGRx CENTER NEAR YOU

LearningRx, Inc. is one of the Top 45 fastest growing new franchises in the United States. LearningRx training produces unmatched gains in cognitive learning and reading skills. The needs are real and growing, and prime, protected territories are still available for franchise opportunities. If you are interested in helping to bring cognitive skills training to your community, visit **www.learningrx-franchise.com** or call **(800) 535-5441** to learn more about the LearningRx Training Center opportunity.